ORGANIZATIONAL PERFORMANCE ART

ORGANIZATIONAL PERFORMANCE

ART

HOLDING SPACE FOR JOY AND POSSIBILITY

Alissa Schwartz

IMPELLER PRESS

different.⬚track
This book is made possible with support from Different Track Productions, a program of the non-profit organization Continuum Culture & Arts.
https://www.continuumculture.org

Cover and text design by Patrick Barber
Set in Meno Text, Capital Gothic, and Headline Gothic
Display titles created from scans of letterpress-printed wood type

ISBN-13: 9798988013358
Library of Congress Control Number: 2023945014

Impeller Press books are published by Patrick Barber in Portland, Oregon, which was built on top of village sites of the Multnomah, Wasco, Cowlitz, Kathlamet, Clackamas, Chinook, Tualatin, Kalapuya, Molalla, and many other tribes who made their homes here. Today, members of these tribes and others are part of our community in the Portland metro area. We honor them with this land acknowledgement, and we give 5% of our gross sales to support Indigenous communities and the Landback movement. Please visit landback.org for more information on the Landback movement.

This book is printed to order, just for you. Thanks to this remarkable manufacturing technology, tiny publishers like myself are able to make books widely available without the cost or waste of excess books.

Printed and distributed by Ingram Publishing Services

impellerpress.com

IMPELLER

This book is dedicated to all the culture builders who play in the realm of the unseen. May we help the world survive and thrive.

This book is also dedicated to my Mom and Dad, April and Alan Schwartz. Sitting around the Shabbes table, you were my first teachers in hosting and holding space.

CONTENTS

FORE-FOREWORD

I REMEMBER SWEEPING MY ARMS UP TO FORM A BIG CIRCLE, crouching up and down, and humming. This movement and sound embodied who I was in that moment—both how I felt and how I was showing up. I walked around the room greeting other people with my full body gesture, and they shared theirs with me. It was a different way to get to know myself and each other, and the physicality of it was transformative and joyful. This was my first taste of Organizational Performance Art, led by Alissa Schwartz.

Over the last two decades, I've supported over 400 organizations, networks, and foundations on shared leadership, equity transformation, resiliency, and systems change that build power toward the liberation of all living beings. Growing up, I was a theater geek and loved playing games that I now know had their origins in environmental theater. As part of social justice activist collectives, we also used Augusto Boal's Theater of the Oppressed activities for political education and other visual and performing arts practices to call attention to injustice. But later, as an organizational development consultant, I had limited the use of art to team building exercises and icebreakers.

With the full body gesture activity, I realized that Alissa was offering a fresh framework for working with groups, a framework that recognized the many ways to engage the body through theater and somatics. That opened up new possibilities for me to support people in knowing themselves, each other, their organization, and the systems within which they're embedded. I realized that this visceral knowledge can be used for relationship-building, learning and reflection, program design and innovation, training and education, organizational restructuring, conflict resolution, and so much more. I also felt empowered to draw on the different lineages and traditions of heart-mind-body practices as I accompanied groups in strengthening their capacity.

Now I incorporate grounding rituals into meetings, use poetry and drawing to unleash creativity in strategy development, create embodied activities for people to learn, hold space for a range of emotions during generative conflict, and so much more.

Organizational Performance Art is grounded in the body and also is more than the body. For me, Organizational Performance Art is a metaphor for tending to the complexity of an organization as a container for collective sense-making and action. How can we see all the parts of an organization—the dynamics among its people and the whole of the organization—at once? Like potters on a wheel, how can we shape this container toward collective thriving and liberation? But unlike potters, how do we do this in a way that engages people not as clay being molded but as self-determined agents co-creating their future in the face of uncertainty?

The dominant ways that we work today are often oppressive and insufficient in achieving collective liberation. Organizations need to be transformed. Many alternatives grounded in ancestral wisdom are (re)emerging and finally becoming seen as the valid and powerful options for change efforts that they have always been. *Organizational Performance Art: Holding Space for Joy and Possibility* is one of these critical offerings and is unique in tying together so many threads—from performance art to spirituality to social justice. I have used the lens and techniques of Organizational Performance Art to guide groups in their transformation, and I invite you to play with these ideas. Try them out. Invent new techniques. With a bit of creativity and joy, the possibilities are limitless.

—SUSAN MISRA, Principal of Aurora Commons and
co-author of *Influencing Complex Systems Change*

WHY WRITE?

Why write a book? Shouldn't work be its own justification?...If this book has value, it is because in it I do something that I cannot do in "the work."...Although my ideas revolve around the work,...other things have entered as well....My studies of anthropology, social psychology, psychoanalysis, and gestalt therapy are the bases of my belief that performance theory is a social science.

RICHARD SCHECHNER[1]

WHY WRITE A BOOK? THAT IS THE QUESTION THEATER director and performance studies professor Richard Schechner poses in the foreword to his book *Environmental Theater*, a work that has stirred me for more than thirty years and is one of the inspirations and muses for writing *this* book. Like Schechner, I took the liberty of writing my own foreword and used the same question "why write a book?" to share my influences and the context within which I write.

I decided to write about my work, because the work itself wasn't fully conveying what I wanted to express. In recent years, an additional something beyond my work called to me. It knocked at my door and whispered to be taken seriously: "Write. Create. Add your voice."

The last time I took on a massive writing project was my doctoral dissertation,[2] around 2007, between babies. Sometimes I call it my third child. It was an examination of the interior world of social workers who work with children in foster care. Talking with these workers was one of the experiences that drove my interest in developing a consultation practice that focuses on building positive and equitable organizational culture. Since 2011, I have consulted with nonprofit, social justice, and philanthropic organizations and communities, facilitating individual and group processes for transformational growth and culture building.

Like Schechner, I will also list formative influences of my work and life. They include social constructionist theory, working with Bread and Puppet Theater, studying and practicing performance art, immersing myself in the documentation of experimental ensemble theater work from the 1960s and '70s, studying and practicing social work and organizational psychology, and engaging in yoga, meditation, and shamanic journeying.

After a decade of consulting, it seemed that I was ready for my fourth child, a literary journey through the theories, practices, influences, and adventures that inform my work. It's my love child, really. A project I share with the world, born of a deep desire to understand how my first love, performance, informs my work and life.

This book expands the concepts and practices of avant-garde theater and performance art, applying them to organizational and community settings. It is the story of how I came to call my work Organizational Performance Art. It is structured and conceptualized as a series of interconnected chapters that begin with my definition of Organizational Performance Art and travel through the various historical, theoretical, and practice influences in the world of performance that contribute to my work, including avant-garde theater and social constructionism.

I characterize an artistic sensibility as the embodiment of a high tolerance for ambiguity and emergence; understanding and playing with the social construction of reality; and working from a place of joy, expansiveness, and possibility. Most artists, narrowly defined, already know how to address the uncertainties in their lives with creativity. They're resilient and critical and fierce. This is a stance I strive to embody in my personal and professional practices. It's needed even more now, as we deal with massive social, political, and environmental trauma at the individual, institutional, and systemic levels. An artistic stance toward organizational change invites creativity, positivity, interconnectedness, and collaboration.

The core force that propels my journey, both in theater and in organizational consulting, is a deep yearning for communal thriving and liberation. Organizational Performance Art does not just change organizations; it is a way of holding space for joy and possibility, harnessing imagination and a willingness to dance with the unknown in service to social justice and equity.

Organizational Performance Art is performative.
Organizational Performance Art is social constructionist.
Organizational Performance Art is shamanic.
It is holding space.
It is creating connective tissue.
It is a deep, visceral dance with the mysterious universe.

A note about the attention I give in this writing to white male theater directors: During my formative years of making theater, when I was in my early 20s, I studied the work of experimental and avant-garde theater artists from the '60s and '70s. This included becoming well acquainted with the work of women and people of color; however, like most people living in the United States, white and otherwise, my studies and life were—and still are—nested within racist institutions and systems that privilege white people. The white male theater directors I write about had the social capital and resources to be able to do their work and have it well documented. This is not always the case for women and artists of color. I am not apologetic about what my heart loves, and I also am clear-eyed about the challenging issues of erasure that come with having been influenced by and writing disproportionately about white male artists. While much of my consulting work focuses on building anti-racist culture, the issue of white supremacy culture within the world of theater is most directly taken up in this book in my writing about Bread and Puppet Theater, with whom I have had ongoing, deep, and meaningful interaction.

ORGANIZATIONAL PERFORMANCE ART

"ORGANIZATIONAL PERFORMANCE ART" IS THE NAME I HAVE given to the consulting work I do. This term employs three words—"organizational," "performance," and "art"—in unexpected fashion. It includes pairings—"organizational performance" and "organizational art"—that relate to the larger concepts of performance and art, respectively. And the three words, when brought together, dance with the world of performance art. In this chapter I break down Organizational Performance Art into the three paired terms that reside within it—"organizational performance," "organizational art," and "performance art"—before looping back and taking on the full concept. The outcome, I can tell you now, is liberation and thriving.

ORGANIZATIONAL PERFORMANCE

"Performance" is a commonly used term in the field of organizational consulting and management. In that context, performance often refers to the actual impact organizations have on the world, and it is generally compared to prior intentions set in advance. Organizational performance is also dependent on individual and team performance. Folks may get annual performance reviews to see how they're measuring up against predetermined individual goals, and staff members who produce high quality work can be considered high performers. Team performance focuses on how well a team produces agreed-upon outputs, and high performing teams are of real value, as well. It is a basic given in the world of nonprofit organizational change and management that the purpose for improving individual, group, and organizational behavior, systems, and culture is to influence organizational performance, the impact an organization has on the world.

The reliance on the term "performance" in the world of organizational change and management is indicative of something much larger at play, however. Organizational performance is, of course, an application of the broader concept of performance. Theater director and performance studies academic Richard Schechner divides human existence into four activities: being, doing, showing doing, and explaining showing doing.[3] While he describes "being" as existence itself, "doing" is any and all activity, and "showing doing" is "pointing to, underlining, and displaying" doing. Performing occurs when there is either doing or showing doing. Explaining showing doing is, in Schechner's case, writing about performance. For me, it is writing about Organizational Performance Art.

Most activities we engage in, other than the core ones required for our beingness, such as respiration, ingestion, elimination, and rest, involve performing. They involve doing and showing doing. We are always performing different versions of ourselves, depending on the setting we are in. We dress, hold our bodies, and talk differently with our colleagues and supervisors, compared to when we are with friends and family. We present ourselves differently to ourselves, with our lovers, with our friends, to our parents, and to our grandparents. The workplace is a stage on which we perform, just as is any other setting.

Here is what I think:

Thinking is performing
Writing is performing
Loving is performing
Mourning is performing
Remembering is performing
Pleasing is performing
Work is performing

Sometimes, participants of group processes I have facilitated question the value I hold of bringing one's full, authentic self to an organization or community. They reserve parts of themselves for their private lives and do not want to share of themselves fully in an organizational setting. In fact, I see no conflict here. Recognizing that we are performative everywhere we go and that our performance changes depending on the context we find ourselves in allows us to embrace the different selves we are and not feel bifurcated.

This reconceptualization of organizational performance is linked to many other topics related to performance that I touch on in this book, including social constructionist theory and shamanic journeying, and, of course, environmental theater and performance art. Invoking a broader understanding of the concept of performance allows for a wider range of principles, tools, and practices that can be accessed within an organizational context. It allows for wholeness, breath, and play.

ORGANIZATIONAL ART

In our racialized capitalist society, where value is defined by the ability to make money, art is generally consumed for entertainment and not considered worthy of investment, except for the rare artist and their work which has been deemed to be of financial value. This means that the term "art" is often associated with what cannot produce financial value. This understanding of art financially marginalizes most visual, media, and performing artists, and at the same time it disenfranchises people working in other fields by not allowing their work to be considered art. Organizational consulting is generally not considered art, but it can and should be.

I define art as the application of creativity, innovation, and curiosity to any given function. The term "organizational art" centers an artistic approach to organizational change. While the term "art" has been taken up by many in my field, it is often used in a narrow, limited way. Calling something the "art of xxx" applies the imprimatur of "art," as it is traditionally understood, on whatever is being described. It doesn't, however, put a stake in the ground and get clear on what exactly is meant by art.

PERFORMANCE ART

This may be the most difficult pairing of terms. For many, it brings up associations of suffering through inscrutable, anything-goes performances, ones that are considered less rigorous or meaningful when compared to art on a wall, a play, choreography, or a musical score. Performance Art makes use of a wide range of art forms and activities, often using non-traditional art spaces. It is human bodies doing something over time and framing it as art. Performance art historian RoseLee Goldberg defines the term as "live art by artists" who take "life as its subject."[4]

While Performance Art is often associated with performance that has developed since the 1970s or so, it has its roots in early 20th century avant-garde visual art. Its ancestral lineage includes Happenings, live events created by visual artists in the 1950s and '60s. Allan Kaprow's book on the subject traces the development of Happenings to visual artists' work on Assemblages in the earlier part of the 20th century.[5] With Assemblages, visual artists created cultural objects from found items. Eventually, they grew their work to human-scale Environments that allowed viewers to walk in, around, and through them. Happenings evolved from this tradition and added an overt performative element.

Instead of (or in addition to) having physical objects be the center of viewers' attention, people were utilized as artistic material. Viewers were encouraged to interact both with the physical environments as well as the people/performers inhabiting these environments. In fact, with Happenings, there are often no spectators. Everyone is a participant.

An organizational application of Performance Art is part of the Assemblage–Environments–Happenings continuum. Organizational applications of Performance Art use a few rules regarding human interaction to guide the behavior of a group. By providing simple directives that yield unexpected outcomes, an organizational application of Performance Art invites and frames participants' interactions as consciously performative rather than unconsciously so. Consider the following instructions from different participatory conversational methodologies and structures that I utilize:

- Discuss with your table partners a given question for thirty minutes. In the next round, find new table partners to discuss a new question. (World Café[6])

- Stay with a discussion group only if you have something to contribute or learn. (Open Space[7])

- Sit in a circle. Talk only when holding the talking piece. (Circle Practice[8])

These directives live in a similar space as those that Kaprow gave in his 1959 work *18 Happenings in 6 Parts*,[9] such as when a bell rings you may move to a different room. They have a common, eye-opening, sometimes giddy effect on their participants. People follow directives and interact with each other in novel ways.

I am choosing to widen the term Performance Art, just as I have widened the terms "performance" and "art," separately, to inform organizational change work. Performance Art is art, broadly defined, that centers live human process. As I apply the term to organizational work, Performance Art invites in a specific stance that centers live, emergent human process as the artistic medium.

The effects of an organizational application of Performance Art can be liberatory and long-lasting. They can enliven communities and organizations beyond the confines of time and space allotted for an event. In fact, this is a major distinction between an organizational application of Performance Art and their artistic forebears. While an organizational application of Performance Art starts in a room, its effect on a community or organization may ripple on, without end.

ORGANIZATIONAL PERFORMANCE ART

Organizational Performance Art is performance art; it utilizes carefully designed live, participatory processes that are out of time with the regular routines and processes of an organization and the public it serves. Organizational Performance Art is also organizational art; it is the witnessing and working with the internal functioning of a group, utilizing an artistic sensibility that is centered on creatively working with emergence. And Organizational Performance Art's raison d'être is to positively influence organizational performance, in the myriad of ways that performance can be conceptualized.

The term Organizational Performance Art centers a performative, or theatrical, frame to foster deeper connection and authenticity. I facilitate—direct—organizational participants—actors—in a meeting space—and time—that is artificial, different, and separate from the normal workday. And within that very artifice, I invite people to bring their full, authentic selves forward in a way that can be worked back into their regular day-to-day workspace and encounters. It is a theatrical employment of artifice in service to an authentic end, that of organizational transformation.

Transformation is not change for the sake of doing something different. Transformation is powerful, meaningful change in service to positive social thriving and liberation. Thriving is moving in the direction of actualization. It is flourishing. Liberation is a freeing from oppression by people who have historically taken or been granted power over others because of their social identities. These include (but are not limited to) race, gender, sexuality, age, ability, religion, nationality, family composition, and education.

Organizational Performance Art supports organizational thriving and liberation and inspires the following questions for my field and the world at large, questions taken up both directly and indirectly throughout this book:

- How can we—organizations and the people who support them— move from a place where an organization's internal members (e.g., staff, volunteers, board) are oriented toward performing for external stakeholders (e.g., service and product recipients, funders, politicians) to a place that is more collaborative, real, present, emergent, uncertain, and fluid?

- How can the work at retreats and special meetings that examine, practice, and set intentions for positively transforming organizational culture inform a new way to be back in the day-to-day functioning of an organization and life at large?

- How can Organizational Performance Artists use illusion (the artifice of a meeting or retreat) in the service of dis-illusion? (That is, how can we develop the connective tissue to bridge from artifice back to day-to-day functioning that has been transformed by the artifice?)

- Why is the norm to *perform* at work and thus not show up as our full selves? Why is there no invitation to yoke together passion and responsibility, to initiate, to live?

- Why are we so afraid of uncertainty and emergence?

At the heart of the work of an Organizational Performance Artist is the holding of space in service to communal thriving and liberation. Holding space involves an emptying out of oneself to be emotionally, spiritually, psychologically, and mentally present for and attuned with others. While I am aware, when I am holding space, of how my body feels, what my thoughts are, and what emotions I am experiencing, I am focused on using my presence as invitation for people to first feel and then share their own presence. It is part modeling, part emptying out, part invitation.

Organizational Performance Art holds space for joy and possibility. It holds space for sitting with uncertainty, playing with new ideas and practices, and co-creating emergently. Helping people to develop greater tolerance for sitting in the discomfort of not knowing what is next is one of its central practices. Riding a wild, unknown wave and not being subsumed by it invites people to engage all of their senses, be receptive to what is going on for them internally, and stay open to exchange with the rest of the world. It softens the bounds between people and invites in possibility. It is a precondition for co-creation, and co-creation is a precondition for communal thriving and liberation.

I offer a few parameters that encourage people to fully manifest and bring their best selves forward. Performing, whether it is among actors in a theater or with colleagues in a social change organization, is about the art of being. Organizational Performance Art, holding-space art, allows this to happen. Two community members who participated in a series of meetings I facilitated described their experience. One said, "When you arrive and sit with us, our conversation, our presence, is electrified." The other added, "We go deep, quickly, with a lot of trust, and we're not necessarily all trusting people."

Organizational Performance Art is holding space. Holding space is witnessing. Witnessing is performing. Performing is playing. Playing is dancing with joy and possibility. Dancing with joy and possibility is delighting. Delighting is co-creating the conditions for liberation and thriving. Co-creating the conditions for liberation and thriving is what it's all about.

These concepts are deeply explored in this book.

PERFORMANCE

STORIES

PERFORMANCE IS MY FIRST STORY. MY FIRST STORY WEAVES through my later stories. My later stories are also performance, Organizational Performance Art.

I was a very theatrical and attention-grabbing kid. I loved seeing myself and being seen. Some of my first memories are of performing and dancing, for both myself and for others. My grandmother gave me a little Kodak 110 camera when I was about eight years old. I used it to take pictures of myself, vamping in the long mirror on her closet door, striking glamorous pose after glamorous pose. Even earlier, when my parents' friends came over to dinner, I clamored to perform, to be on stage. And to direct, if I was allowed to.

Aside from taking the unsurprising ballet lessons from age six to twelve, I also attended many theatrical and musical performances with my parents. They were subscribing members of St. Louis' Theatre Project Company, and we attended many plays performed by their ensemble in the basement of Union Station, an abandoned, cavernous train station. When I was about eleven years old, I attended a play called *A Day in the Death of Joe Egg*.[10] It was about a young person living in a vegetative state from cerebral palsy. The play was horrifying, disturbing, riveting. I only wondered how that kid got their acting gig.

I was smitten with a prominent local actress and founding member of the company. Her name was Fontaine Syer. Her ability to breathe life into many a different role awed me. I remember seeing her face on a cereal box, presumably a commercial gig she had accepted to supplement her company wages. I complained to my parents that she was a sellout, not yet knowing about the pernicious social, political, and economic pressures that artists endure when trying to support themselves in the United States.

In high school, there were the annual musicals, which didn't do much for me and were directed by the yearbook teacher. Our school was also lucky enough to have an acting and directing teacher who was the beloved leader of an artsy group of kids. Her name was Mary Jane Hogue, and I spent hours and hours and hours with her in her basement classroom. She didn't have nearly as much clout in the school as the yearbook teacher, but she was our star.

After I graduated high school, I went off to college with the intent to direct theater. I was astonishingly underwhelmed with the department, however, whose sole purpose seemed to be to feed the enormous egos of its white male faculty and churn out capable actors for their boring living-room dramas. I was told that the experimental work I was doing was not actually directing, and I felt like I was suffocating. I needed more expansive horizons.

ENCOUNTERING BREAD AND PUPPET THEATER

After my first year in college, I was invited by folks from Oddfellows Playhouse, the community children's theater that I was working with, to go with them to Vermont to see Bread and Puppet Theater. I had never heard of the group, and gamely joined. Founded in 1963 by Peter

Schumann, Bread and Puppet Theater was born on the streets of New York City, where they engaged in protest theater against the Vietnam War. Bread and Puppet later settled into their current home, farmland in Glover, Vermont, where they have performed for the last several decades countless politicized shows and spectacles.

Bread and Puppet blew my mind. I saw a passion play on their meadow for Archbishop Oscar Romero, a liberation theologist who upheld the rights of poor and disenfranchised El Salvadorans and was murdered in 1980 by a right-wing death squad. I crisscrossed from meadow to forest and back to meadow again, taking in sideshows on topics that ranged from Palestinian rights to deforestation. I nestled in among the thousands gathered in the former gravel pit, now natural amphitheater, for the Domestic Resurrection Circus.

At the opening of the Circus, puppeteers ran from out of the woods onto the ring, wildly waving flags, while a band of traditional and junk instruments played and audience members enthusiastically clapped and grasshoppers leapt about. Puppeteers playing garbagemen and washerwomen were the heroes of the day, cleaning up after acts that were both entertaining and highly political. This was agitprop that married the land. Here were hills, trees, fields, and sky intermingling with enormous puppets, stilters, banners, and bread. Here were manifestos and conflagrations, sacred harp singing, and funky band mashups. Here was a highly realized manifestation of marrying craft, place, and social vision. It was a dream come true. No, I didn't even know one could dream this way.

How can I describe the just-so feeling of satisfaction, awe, gratitude, and pleasure that rippled through me when I beheld a giant Mother Earth puppet in the distance—a serene face in browns and blacks, perhaps ten feet high, making her way ever so slowly through the gently rolling green fields toward us? Puppeteers dressed in white supported her, wheeling her visage and holding aloft her floating arms and body—silky white cloth that flowed around her, catching the wind, billowing. Her slow movement forward was nearly imperceptible. The humans supporting her were so small, the vision for peace and unity in the world enormous.

How can I share the feeling of holding a small piece of sourdough rye bread, baked in a clay oven right on the field, slathered with an aioli of oil and garlic? The tang of the bread, the pungency of the aioli, the just-rightness of receiving the same meal as hundreds, thousands of pilgrims. Of sweating garlic.

After that first thrill of discovery, I worked with Bread and Puppet the next summer. I was—frankly—fairly miserable much of the time. While I stilted, sewed burlap costumes, peeled and chopped an unfathomable number of garlic cloves, stage-managed for Peter, and—of course—worked puppets small and large, I bridled at the severe hierarchies that kept me at the bottom. Old-timers were favored over newcomers, men over women. I had my own ideas and strong directorial urges, and as a young, female, newcomer, I was summarily shut down, ordered not to do my sideshow on environmental preservation and feminism. So, I sulked. And continued my journey.

DIRECTING COLLABORATION

In 1990, during my senior year in college, I created and directed a site-specific ensemble performance titled *Made in the CFA* [Center for the Arts]. The work, as well as its documentation, is so deeply influenced by the work of Peter Schumann, as well as that of theater director André Gregory, that it's hard for me, more than thirty years later, to untangle what's mine, what's theirs, and what's ours.

I first came across the theater work of André Gregory when I was drinking up any documentation I could get my hands on of experimental ensemble theater work from the 1960s and '70s. Wesleyan's library was my sanctuary, and I pored over old copies of *TDR: The Drama Review* and searched shelves, book by book, for titles of interest. That's how I stumbled upon *Alice in Wonderland: The Forming of a Company and the Making of a Play.*[11] It was an utter revelation to me, and I repeatedly checked it out from the art library where it was housed. With its rich black and white prints by Richard Avedon, it was categorized as a photography book. I was mesmerized—the text, the images, the intensity. In addition to the captivating photographs, there were interviews by Doon Arbus (photographer Diane Arbus' daughter) with each of the seven ensemble members.

Gregory's method of directing involved working with a group to develop a performance over a very long time. His directing was subtle, creating a space for actors to play and interact, and then using his sensibilities to select and structure the array of possibilities that had been developed. Gregory's directing approach, like Organizational Performance Art, was to hold space for possibility and encourage creative emergence. I wanted to use a similar process in my theater work.

The students performing in *Made in the CFA* were not theater majors. I was repelled by both my college's theater professors and their sycophants. The theater students felt plasticky, pretentious, and robotic, sucking up to the white male faculty and their enormous egos. Although I'm not sure I would have been able to articulate it at the time, I was looking for a certain kind of energetic in my performers, that of being open to emergence, co-creation, and playfulness. I wanted to work with people who trusted we had the right people for the project and could create something meaningful together. I cared more about who each individual was as a person, warts and all, than any traditionally defined acting or performing abilities they might have. The *Made in the CFA* performers were students of social sciences and religion, visual art, and dance.

The only time our group could meet to work together was at seven in the morning. In the cold New England dawn, we donned our jackets, rubbed our hands together for warmth, and played, messed around, tried out different things, and shaped a work together.

Made in the CFA ran for several hours, in and out of a series of connected arts buildings on my college's campus. It was structured along the lines of the epic vision of Bread and Puppet's Circus weekends of the 1980s, with sideshows, circus, pageant, and oratorio performances happening all day and evening all over their farm in Vermont. *Made in the CFA* had a collaboratively created opening part; solo sideshows happening simultaneously throughout the complex; a group piece I wrote, directed, and performed in; and a collaborative closing. The group piece was a retelling of real and mythical women's access to power, featuring the Greek mythological character Ariadne, the women who followed Charles Manson, and Lewis Carroll's Alice. The overalls we wore were made from quilted moving blankets—a thrifty shortcut to get to a similar textural quality I was lusting after from the costumes of Gregory's *Alice*.

Inspired by *Alice*, I documented the work and its process in the form of an artist book, with text, photographs, and unique visual elements in each of the seven copies I made. I interviewed each performer about their experience rehearsing and performing. Many performers talked about how my conceptualization and emphasis on an end-product—the performance—had undermined what they had expected from being involved in an emergent, co-creative process.[12]

> Kate: I got frustrated that so much of the time was spent performing, even for one another, as opposed to talking things out.

> Dalton: There could have been a lot more collaboration if you had given us things to work on, specific ideas to have prepared for the next time we met.

> Rebecca: We kept wanting to condense the collaborative stuff.

> Mike: Here's how I imagined it before we began; I was sort of disappointed it never ended up being that way: I imagined it being really difficult. I imagined that a group coming together will discover something about themselves and their interactions as people before they try to create something, and that

interaction will bring out the issues which exist between them.... I imagined this balance that everybody has between going with the flow of the whole group and being motivated to put in their own input. This is how I was thinking of *Alice in Wonderland*. These people got together; they were perfectly willing to...be completely physically comfortable with one another, get through all that tension that exists between people. Maybe that's what's inherent in collaboration, bringing out people's emotions and not trying to make everything pleasant all the time.

Dalton: Both nights [of improvisational rehearsal] there was a point where...no one was worried about what was going on. And I thought those moments were great, and I have as much difficulty as anyone else in letting that continue to exist. But I also think we didn't work enough with it.

I was hearing from the performers that my intentions had not entirely matched what actually occurred during the process of creating and performing *Made in the CFA*. I felt shame, confusion, and frustration that my director self didn't know how to dance well with my collaborator self. During those early years of professional identity development, I did not know how to reconcile my two strong drives: directing and co-creating. They felt in conflict with each other. How could I reconcile my interest in emergent and creative group process with my strong tendencies and ability to direct, shape, and mold? As I interviewed my performers, I mused about what pure collaboration, without direction, might look like:

Alissa: I wonder if you only had those kinds of rehearsals, would you be able to have a final product to present to the public? Would you want to? For this project, I wanted to publicly present a vision directed by me.... I have a fantasy called "collaboration glory." I'm interested in locking myself in a room for a few years with a group of people and seeing what happens, playing and not worrying about the end product but focusing on establishing deep trust.... How can I unite my perfect vision of collaboration with reality?

PERFORMING HARD

After I graduated from college, without fully articulating it to myself, I began to move away from being dependent on others to fulfill my artistic vision and became more focused on solo performance. Without the resources of a university—and my parents—I stopped, for the moment, exploring co-creative process.

I created performances that continued to be site-specific, but required fewer people and resources to pull off. *Environmental Dinner #1* (1991) was performed just twice by my partner Andrew and me. It was a site-specific installation in our apartment that was played to about twenty friends each night. Andrew and I were not seen for most of the piece, staying "backstage" behind tunnels and rooms that audience members accessed. As participants climbed the two flights of exterior stairs and entered our apartment, they were met with a directive to dress in white shirts found in the refrigerator, divest themselves of their jewelry and other belongings, and stick their hands through an opening in a wall, where we washed them.

Next, participants crawled through a cardboard tunnel that assigned them to one of two rooms, each a different installation. One room was pitch black with soft, shredded paper on the floor. The other one was beach-like, candlelit, with sand and water. Both rooms had dinner—spaghetti—waiting to be consumed.

It was part social experiment, part happening. Andrew and I had surreptitiously recorded people's comments as they were waiting on the exterior stairway to be processed. The recording was then fed back to them as they were dining in their separate rooms. At one point a participant realized what was going on and made a lot of noise to cover up the private badmouthing of another audience member that had been caught on tape.

Andrew and I made brief, silent appearances at each room, but we were largely unseen, controlling the experience. The first night, people found a way to enter each other's room and ignored the injunction to stay put. The second night, Andrew and I secured the entrances to each room so you could exit but not enter the other space. We left and went out to eat.

Europe (1994) was a solo performance installation that I performed about a dozen times to audiences of two people each. It was a meditation on historical social anarchist movements and living experiments. Andrew decamped to a nearby café for several hours as I set and reset the piece, performing the half-hour show a half-dozen times over the course of an evening. Audience members sat in a small, enclosed space in our living room constructed from PVC piping and plastic sheeting while I performed and manipulated various objects behind and above them.

My performance art was not making an impact beyond my personal network, however, and I found myself wanting a way to play on a bigger, more public stage. My next few years began with a year of international travel where I performed street theater with Andrew for thousands of people in Mexico and Central America. Our work was a protest against the celebration of the 500th anniversary of Columbus arriving in the Americas and of the first Iraq war.

During the second half of our travels, we went to Eastern Europe and Scandinavia. In college, I had been turned on to avant-garde Polish theater and knew about the holy communion that existed between audience and performers, using symbol and subterfuge to protest against governmental repression. By the time we arrived in 1993, the fall of the Berlin Wall, the end of the Soviet Union, and the embrace of a free market economy had a profound effect on the experimental theater community. New personal freedoms were sweeping Poland, but for the first time since Communist rule began people were compelled to eke out their existence under the invisible hand of a free market. As in Mexico and Central America, we encountered impoverished people selling trinkets to travelers. There was simply no experimental theater to be found.

In Wroclaw, we knocked on the doors of Jerzy Grotowski's Polish Laboratory Theatre, inactive since the 1980s when Grotowski had moved his theater home to Italy. The Lab housed the group's archives, however, and we were treated to an incredible private screening of their work from the 1960s. Despite us having never seen their work live nor understanding what they were saying in Polish, their compelling, visceral work on extermination camps and repressive governmental regimes still ranks among the most provocative theater I have ever witnessed.

When we returned from our travels, we lived in Seattle, where I performed with a local group that utilized Augusto Boal's Theater of the Oppressed participatory and problem-solving techniques with street youth and other groups. Yet, I was in crisis about my trajectory as a performance artist. The world of experimental theater and performance was under terrible social, economic, and political pressure. This was a few short years after the 1990 scandal surrounding the NEA Four, a group of four individual performance artists who had their funding revoked by the National Endowment for the Arts who considered their work obscene. This was the beginning of funding drying up for performance artists, and I worried that unless I had the drive, luck, and talent of one of the very few people who would be getting funding and recognition, it was highly unlikely that I could ever support myself doing the work that interested me.

SOCIAL WORKING

I always had a strong drive to interact with and impact the larger world, and this drive came to a head with an existential crisis in my mid-20s that resulted in my transitioning away from theater practice to social work. At the time, this shift felt like a painful concession to having to survive in a flawed world where I was not able to figure out how I could support myself as an artist.

Having worked with runaway and throwaway youth and volunteering for a crisis hotline, I found that I had the temperament and interest in providing direct support to people in need. I decided to go to graduate school and study social work. While the field had none of the electric energy that performance held for me, I thought it offered a way to practice my social justice values and have greater impact in the world. Unfortunately, I realized after I began my studies that much of the social work practice I was learning about and engaging in had been co-opted to preserve the status quo of social and economic systems rather than disrupt them. I was taught to assess the parental skills of families living in poverty rather than to swim upstream and find ways to end conomic inequality.

My first post-masters job, which was also my first job in New York City after moving there from Seattle, was working with an advocacy organization for homeless people. We were the court-appointed independent investigator of conditions in the public adult shelter system spread across four of the five boroughs. A large part of my job involved inspecting facilities alongside the City's inspector and ensure that they were being thorough in their work. I was explicitly instructed by my organization to maintain an adversarial relationship with the City's inspector; however, I found it anathema to develop a relationship built on presumed contention and found that cordial, friendly interactions resulted in the desired outcome of an accurate documentation of the shelters' conditions.

People in my organization made fun of my approach and accused me of flirting with the inspector. While I was keenly interested in improving the housing conditions for the most vulnerable of New Yorkers, I found the interpersonal dynamics among people in this organization to be unfriendly, competitive, and mean. In addition to running around the city flushing toilets and looking for signs of rodents, I studied the interpersonal dynamics happening around and with me, preparing myself for a future of supporting organizational culture building.

After about a year, I left the organization and was hired for a newly created position in a nonprofit organizational consulting practice, only to be let go six weeks later. I was told that the external organizational consultant working with them said that it was a mistake to have created my position! I never believed that, and always wondered what it was about me that they felt wasn't a good fit. I imagined they had hoped for someone with less backbone, who could be more easily molded into their way of doing things, but it's also entirely possible that I overpersonalized what happened and they just really didn't have their act together.

Next, I joined an organization where I provided technical assistance to food pantries and soup kitchens throughout New York City. The sluggishness of working within a band-aid organization that seemed almost proud of being underresourced and understaffed drove me nuts.

PERFORMING SOFT

That's when I went back to school to study organizational behavior and psychology and to get my doctorate. I studied and worked with faculty in social work, business, and organizational leadership. I loved designing and conducting independent research. My dissertation was an examination of the interior world of social workers who work with children in foster care.[13] I wanted to know what made them engage in work that was so poorly understood and valued by society. What kept them going? I conducted twenty-five in-depth interviews with workers from five different organizations and found that despite a nearly universal passion for and commitment to supporting children and their families, the characteristics of the organizations within which they worked, whether they were negative (such as having inadequate training, overwhelming work demands, and lower salaries) or positive (including having good practices in staff recognition and support), had a profound impact on the workers' morale and retention.

After I graduated, I engaged in another round of demoralizing jobs, including engaging in employment-related research with a batch of mean-spirited, competitive academics and serving as the director of program evaluation for another sluggish social service agency. I realized I would never be truly happy or impactful working within a social service organization. I didn't like the focus on band-aid solutions, the organizational dysfunction, the hierarchies, and not being able to use my real gifts. I needed more autonomy, a bigger canvas to paint on, and I was more interested in supporting the internal workings of social change organizations than being part of them.

Friends and family had been telling me for years to consider going into business for myself, but the thought of self-employment panicked all of my financial-stability-seeking buttons. Realizing that I would have only myself to blame for more malaise and frustration if I continued to work jobs that didn't fit me, I faced my demons and started Solid Fire Consulting. It took a few years to build a practice that focused on group process facilitation and culture building, as I initially didn't look strong on paper in those areas.

Over time, I discovered how to adapt many group processes that fascinated me from my theater days and found opportunities to practice them with social change organizations. By choosing to work with people who were not theater performers, I had the added, meaningful challenge to take my practices and wisdoms and gentle and subtle them enough so that they could be received and embraced by people of different walks. I learned to tune in with each new environment as I entered, danced with, and helped support change.

I began to realize that the organizational facilitation and culture change work I was doing was an extension of the ethos and sensibilities of the avant-garde theater work I was fascinated with from the '60s and

'70s. I had found a way to stay centered in my values and serve a broad array of social justice organizations doing important work in the world. I had arrived at that moment of "collaboration glory" that I so yearned for three decades earlier. I may not lock myself in a room with an organization for many months on end, but the principles of co-creation and working with what emerges are at the center of all that I do.

I had come full circle and integrated my performance background into my consulting practice, centering joy and possibility with my clients. I began to describe my work as Organizational Performance Art.

ENCOUNTERING BREAD AND PUPPET AGAIN

In 2013, Andrew and I took our children Ash and Egg to Bread and Puppet in Vermont, the first time for our kids, and the first time in over fifteen years for the two of us. Behind the barn that housed the Museum with its puppets going back to the 1960s, there was a new building I hadn't seen before. When we entered the Papier Maché Cathedral, we were surrounded by brown paper reliefs painted with black details covering every surface—walls, beams, ceiling. We drank in the delicious, low-lit quiet while Peter sawed away on his fiddle and blew on a bottle to cue puppeteers. We watched audiotape rhythmically, magically, cleverly unspooling from boxes and ice melting from spoons suspended over a drum, the plunk-plunk-plunk getting more and more muffled until a puppeteer in a dark blue jumpsuit wiped the drumhead dry. And then the spoons, free of the weight of the melting ice, cantilevered back and struck a dulcimer. It was sublime. The next morning, I woke up with a soft heart, grabbed my journal and wrote a letter to Peter, expressing my gratitude and awe: "That image at the end of *Shatterer*, of all the lanterns rising and falling in the night woods while a puppeteer sings a high-pitched aria and you saw away at bread, cutting it into chunks. I hope it always stays with me."

Four years later, I got over myself enough to actually send the damn letter, and Peter wrote back. He invited me to bring my kids by the bread oven the next time I was there. And I did. And we connected. And my kids fell in love with Bread and Puppet. And we performed in the Circus when they came to New York City that winter. Ash and I breathed together as a buffalo. Egg and I cavorted as rats. We were also opening and closing flag runners, a pig, a devil dancer...

When I reconnected with Peter in 2017, he asked me what I did and whether I was happy. When I told him I helped groups work better together and that I loved doing what I do, he was genuinely happy for me and laughed about how his puppeteers love that group process stuff—that he doesn't truck with it, but he can see how much it benefits them.

I started performing with Bread and Puppet, off and on, during their winter New York City runs. I got to know puppeteers, and I learned from them how things had changed a few short years after my own tumultuous summer with them in 1989. In the mid-'90s, a group of radical feminist puppeteers had had enough of the misogynist crap and staged a disruption—a protest—right in the middle of a Circus! Peter was rattled and things changed.

In 2018, Egg and I performed in the last Circus on the farm for that summer. Egg was a green communal troll. I was a blue grasshopper that tried desperately to keep up with her fellow insects, running and hopping around the ring and behind the audience, making full use of the natural amphitheater. It was hard work, and sometimes I didn't know how we fit, and other times I connected with puppeteers, mostly ones that were a little more on the margins, like us.

And smack dab in the middle of the cheering, happy crowd was the love of my life. Andrew. Filming and cheering us on. I was looking out from the ring that I looked longingly into thirty years before. I looked out from the ring at my love whom I met thirty years ago, the very same weekend that I encountered the magic of Bread and Puppet.

And Egg and I ran with our flags, following each other and other puppeteers in and out and around the Circus ring. We ran with the flags that have opened and closed the Circus over its many decades, bright-colored banners hoisted high, illustrating and invoking the elementals: brother toothbrush, brother sky, sister coffee, brother frying pan, sister garden, sister wind, brother mountain, sister water. We ran and ran and ran and ran flags. Really, there's nothing more joyful for me than running flags at Bread and Puppet. It makes my heart burst wide, wide, wide open. The clouds, the sky, the fields, the birds, the grasshoppers, the people, the flags.

Because of my mother's death and the COVID-19 pandemic, I didn't perform with Bread and Puppet again until they came to New York City in December of 2021. This time, I chose to participate in a more somber show that was being actively directed by Peter. More than three decades after I first encountered Bread and Puppet, I marveled backstage at how much their culture had changed. The puppeteers were more queer, less white, took more leadership. The social justice issues that Bread and Puppet illuminated were more inclusive, often centering queer folk, women, and people of color. Everyone seemed a lot happier. They still worked hard, were a little insular and cliquish, and looking cool and cute had supplanted machismo, but they were also more welcoming, soft, and—importantly—joyful.

Although his wife Elka had died that summer, I had never seen Peter so full of delight and good humor. Historically a rather taciturn, introverted person, he seemed changed to me, and others agreed. During rehearsals, Peter praised us when we did something pleasing to him, and we worked hard to get things the way he wanted—his waving arms, simultaneous blowing on two horns, and squeaking plastic bottle honks giving us our cues. He was our clownish master and we obeyed.

One of the benefits of visiting and revisiting a group and experiencing it from all different angles (college-age puppeteer, pilgrimage maker in my 20s, 30s, and 40s, puppeteer with Ash and Egg in my 50s) is that you get to see how you change, the group changes, and how the chemistry between those two bodies changes.

It warmed my heart to see Peter, who has had many, many people cross his path over the decades of Bread and Puppet's existence, show genuine pleasure at having me be with the group for the week. At the start of the run, sitting a few rows up in the raked audience seats, I listened to Peter talk on stage. He recognized me, smiled, and gave me a big wave. Later that evening, Peter elbow-bumped me and we chatted for a bit. Little things, but big.

I loved holding cardboard cutouts of chairs six inches from my face, breathing slowly, and giving sideways glances to stay coordinated with my fellow puppeteers. I loved tromping all over with a big red flag, waving and jumping and marching around. I loved forming a sea of blue people bobbing in the ocean. I loved having no clue what the show was really about or actually looked like because I was so deeply immersed in being in sync with others on stage and readable to the audience.

On opening night, as we donned our white clothing, stretched, rested, and waited for the show to begin, I thought to myself, "I think I like the rehearsals even more than the performances." I realized I would miss witnessing Peter in his directorial process, as we would be seeing and hearing him less during the actual performances.

And right before our first performance, I learned that one of the puppeteers was the son of Dic Wheeler, the artistic director of Oddfellows Children's Playhouse. It was Dic who invited me in the summer of 1988 to go with Oddfellows folks on a road trip to Vermont to see Bread and Puppet for the first time, forever influencing me in my aesthetic, ideals, and life choices.

Over the course of the week, I realized I had become an old-timer puppeteer. One of the original old-timers asked me, "Remind me when we first met." I told him it was when I was a college student and he was so much older, and how funny it was that we were the same age now. "Yes, I got younger," he quipped.

The week was such a gift. I got to be in community with puppeteers, newer and more veteran, younger and older, and to find my place among them, once again. Something had definitely shifted within the company and within me, and I found myself happier, more comfortable, and showing up more authentically than I had ever experienced with Bread and Puppet before.

ENVIRONMENTAL THEATER

WHILE WRITING THIS BOOK, I REVISITED EARLY AND ABIDING theater friends in print, to see how they held up, informed, and interacted with my organizational work. In particular, one of Richard Schechner's first books, *Environmental Theater*,[14] had a major impact on me when I was an undergrad, learning and yearning.

Schechner, in fact, is one of my grand-mentors, meaning he gave guidance to someone who guided me. When I was an undergrad, I spent a semester with the Trinity/LaMama Performing Arts Program. It was founded by theater director Leonardo Shapiro who, years earlier, had studied with Schechner at New York University. Part studio classes, part internship, and part attending and critiquing countless performances, the program was a deep immersion in the world of late 1980s performance in New York City. We had tea with Vanessa Redgrave, a private audience with Laurie Anderson, and multi-day workshops with butoh dancers Eiko and Koma and performance artist Karen Finley. I saw works in raw basements and legendary spaces, including the Wooster Group at The Performing Garage, where Schechner had directed The Performance Group in the 1960s and '70s.

At the core of *Environmental Theater* is Schechner's desire to define—and elevate—the practice of Environmental Theater, which he distinguishes from traditional Orthodox Theater. The term "environmental" is not used by Schechner to mean ecology in a narrow sense of interacting biosystems, but instead to signify the value for and use of physical space and group process, beyond the cultural assumptions of how both audience and performers should behave in traditional proscenium theaters.

The table on pages 34 and 35 summarizes the key features that distinguish Environmental Theater from Orthodox Theater. Environmental Theater's defining features are similar to those that distinguish my approach to group process in comparison to traditional group work with organizations. I could easily switch the terms "Orthodox Organizational Work" for Orthodox Theater and "Organizational Performance Art" for "Environmental Theater" and the features listed in the table would be as pertinent to my work as they are to Schechner's. It is the difference between offering sensory activities, conversational structures, and powerful questions to a group and responding to what emerges (Organizational Performance Art) and providing off-the-shelf trainings and by-the-book workshops (Orthodox Organizational Work).

In an organizational context, the term "performers" corresponds to internal members of an organization, including staff, volunteers, and board members, and the term "audience" corresponds to external stakeholders interacting with an organization, including service and product recipients (often referred to by organizations as the "target audience"), funders, and politicians. Orthodox Organizational Work focuses on supporting performers—the internal members of an organization—to please their audience, its external stakeholders. Organizational Performance Art blends the worlds of performers and audience,

ORTHODOX THEATER

Use of traditional spaces, notably proscenium stages

Rigid boundaries between audience and performers

Custom-bound theatrical practices

Scripted work

Concerned with illusion, how performers and audience look

Rehearsal and repetition dependent

Focus is on the end product

Audience does not participate, has private reactions

Audience willingly suspends belief in reality

Production is mimetic of life and method acting is utilized (e.g., actor experiences a character's inner motivation as their own)

Performance is bounded in a predetermined fashion

Purpose of the work: the experience of magic

(Orthodox Organizational Work)

offering processes where staff, service recipients, and funders can be in a room together, co-creating.

With Orthodox Organizational Work, the traditional meeting configuration is rows of people facing presenters, while ones used in Organizational Performance Art can range from people arranged in a circle to small groups scattered about the room and even spilling into the outdoors. The sky's the limit.

In Orthodox Organizational Work, traditional strategic planning processes, with their attempts to foresee the future, are the "rehearsal dependent" approach to organizational planning, while keeping one's purpose and values at the center while responding to all of life's unexpected curveballs is Organizational Performance Art's "preparation dependent" approach.

ENVIRONMENTAL THEATER

Use of alternative spaces, including site specific and constructed ones

Fluid boundaries between audience and performers

Experimental theatrical practices

Emergent, unscripted work

Concerned with functioning, how performers and audience work

Preparation dependent

Focus is on group process and group development

Audience may participate and/or share reactions

Audience's reality is changed

Production is real life and performers' presence and personal experience are valued

Anything that happens is part of the performance

Purpose of the work: the experience of ecstasy

(Organizational Performance Art)

Orthodox Organizational Work's focus on the end product in organizational life means employing a narrow understanding of how to achieve social impact that is not connected to the well-being and functioning of an organization's staff, volunteers, and board. In contrast, Organizational Performance Art is concerned with the internal functioning of an organization. A main premise is that the way people work together affects intended organizational impact.

With Orthodox Organizational Work, trainings and workshops are standalone, separate from the actual work being performed by people. The content is often scripted and can even be mimetic, involving role plays, where participants pretend to be someone else. With Organizational Performance Art, the group work focuses on what is actually happening in a room. It is real and involves experiencing and understanding the actual exchanges among participants.

At the root of both Environmental Theater and Organizational Performance Art practice is a holding of space that honors sitting with the unknown, welcoming participation from all parties, and co-creating emergently. This is what I mean by holding space for joy and possibility in the service of social justice and equity.

I love holding space for a group to work together and witnessing what happens next. When invited to do so, people can get to an amazing place together, one that could not have been predicted. A few years ago I wrote a manifesto about participation. Here is an excerpt:

> The world needs people to connect.
>
> It needs it in board rooms and classrooms and conference halls.
> It needs it in churches and mosques and synagogues.
> It needs it in offices and theaters and living rooms.
> It needs it wherever we show up together.
>
> The stage holds great power to transmit profound messages with clarity. It also creates separation between performers— whether they're on a baseball diamond, a theater proscenium, or a pulpit—and spectators in their corresponding beer-drenched bleachers, rows of plush velvet seats, or long, hard pews.
>
> It's a shanda—a scandalous shame—to go to the trouble to gather people up and then not give them the opportunity to build community. We're not an easy species to herd. Many large-scale events are promoted as community building, yet with their bright, exciting, charismatic speakers taking up most of the airtime, they have fallen short of their target.
>
> We need to meld.
> We need to commune.
> We need a place where the boundaries between us get a little thinner and shimmer.

Inspired by guidelines developed by Schechner to encourage more participation in the theater, I developed a set of facilitator principles that center optimal participation and differentiate the work of Organizational Performance Art from Orthodox Organizational Work:

1. Group processes that are planned in advance and ones that emerge both serve a group.

2. Foster a group's acceptance of sitting in a place of uncertainty.

3. Engage in occasional process checks with a group. Articulate and share what is being done to foster optimal participation.

4. Participants should take responsibility for individual self-care and use their time together to meaningfully co-create.

Below are three stories of Organizational Performance Art that illustrate how these principles work together to strengthen meetings, differentiating them from Orthodox Organizational Work. Each story describes a moment when participants in a meeting took initiative to course-correct what was going on, and how the meetings' facilitators, embodying these principles, were able to adapt and respond. A fourth story illustrates what happens when a facilitator does not embrace these principles.

FROM FORMING COMMUNITY TO DISPERSING TOGETHER

Quaking, shaking, trembling. This is what I remember my body doing as I sat on the last day of an interactive and community-building gathering titled *The Art of Participatory Leadership and Social Change*. I kept staring down fear. The three-day meeting was being hosted by three leaders in an international loose-knit community called the Art of Hosting.[15] The term "hosting" is used rather than "facilitating" to describe the work of holding space for groups.

It was September 2011 in New York City, and the gathering's focus was on how to knit together participatory group processes and social change activism. Something else was going on in New York at the same time, however, that had a parallel focus. Occupy Wall Street, with its protests against the hoarding of wealth in the United States and its use of decentralized leadership, was only about ten days old and had received very little media attention.

One of the gathering's participants, I'll call him Mario, spent much of his free time visiting and interacting with activists at Occupy Wall Street. Another participant, I'll call her Tina, listened with me as Mario described what was going on. We began to realize together that there was an important, historic social moment being birthed at the same time as our gathering. We wanted to learn what was going on at Occupy Wall Street and integrate it into the work we were doing at the gathering.

What this really meant was that we wanted the next day, the final day which had already been planned by our hosts, to have a different flow to it. We wanted to move the day's activities to occur at Occupy Wall Street.

We decided that Mario would speak up and propose a new plan and that Tina and I would back him up. In the morning, Mario spoke. I trembled. It was nerve-racking to watch him face the full group and our very skilled, experienced hosts and state that we wanted to see something different happen. Then Tina spoke. I still trembled. And then I spoke, trembling. And then, something happened that I had not at all anticipated. We three had lost sight that the gathering, including our little "interruption," was being expertly facilitated by three people who beautifully knew how to handle changes of course, momentary blips, and unexpected developments.

Our leaders suggested to our group that we hold a "circle council." This was a consensus decision-making process where, first, each participant would share their thoughts about the proposal to visit Occupy Wall Street. That circle of sharing would be followed by two rounds of providing clarification and generating alternate proposals. Finally, we would vote on the matter.

As the first circle progressed, I heard statements like "I will not go to Wall Street," and my mind immediately went to, "Well, that's a deal breaker," but through the process of iterative circles, new proposals were generated, and I realized that we as a group could come up with a solution that could meet the needs of everyone. Someone proposed that people should choose whether or not they would like to go, that there could be a group that visits Occupy Wall Street and a group that stays. This may seem like an incredibly obvious solution, but it had not remotely occurred to Mario, Tina, or me that we could be in community together while choosing to be in different locales. We had been unconsciously stuck in thinking that as a short-lived, three-day gathering we needed to do everything in unison.

The group, perhaps not surprisingly, decided together that we could, indeed, go different directions for a few hours. This decision resulted in all of the participants getting what they wanted. I learned that skilled, caring hosts serve a community by being not easily rattled, transparently sharing a new process to guide the group through a thorny moment, and that a community can hold multiple individual needs.

Nine of us went to Occupy Wall Street. Many more of us did not go. When we joined up again, we shared our learning with each other, closed the gathering, and said our goodbyes.

FROM SWIMMING IN THE SHALLOWS TO DEEPER DIVING

A colleague and I designed and facilitated a multi-day team-building retreat with an organization focused on social impact investing. Prior to the retreat, we had been working with a large planning group, about seven people who reflected the demographics and roles within the organization. As we were developing the agenda with them and workshopping a few of the activities, we sensed their reticence to engage in anything too deep or risky. There was not a lot of shared trust or honesty within the group, and it would take more than a few planning meetings to change behaviors and norms stemming from an organizational culture built on hierarchical formalities and authoritarianism.

Because they were locked in a culture that was depth avoidant, the planning group could not accept our guidance to build in more authenticity at the retreat or have anticipated needing it. The organization's culture impacted our retreat design, resulting in an agenda that would take the organization only a few baby steps forward in their professed desire to build a more authentic community.

We knew we could push the planning group only so far, so we finalized the agenda, packed our bags, grabbed our markers and facilitation toys and headed to the retreat center. The first day went as we expected. We ran our activities and no major risks were taken. Everyone's energy was fine, but there weren't any profound moments of insight, joy, or connection.

At the end of the first day, my colleague and I checked in with the planning team to see how the day went for them, and they told us they were hungering for the group to go deeper. The retreat was too light and needed more heft. This was exciting news for us to hear, as we realized that our groundwork must have created the conditions for them to be able to feel, recognize, and articulate their emerging needs. It also meant we needed to go back to the drawing board, quickly.

That evening, we redesigned the rest of the retreat. We banged it out, drawing from past facilitation experiences and our ample tool chests of activities, and came up with a plan for how to reframe the rest of our time together. We were thrilled to meet their desire for a course correction toward depth and grateful we had the capabilities to pull it off on such short notice.

That night, I lay in my bed thinking about how, prior to the end of our first day of working together, there was no way for the organization—and the planning group who reflected it—to know what they actually needed at the retreat. The microcosm—the planning group—was a reflection of the macrocosm—the organization. The organization's culture did not allow for deeper, more meaningful interactions, and so in our planning meetings with the microcosm we had designed a rather shallow gathering. It took the microcosm experiencing the low impact of the low-stakes activities on the first day of the retreat to realize a shift was needed. The microcosm shifted so the macrocosm could, as well.

By holding the core purpose of the meeting while creating space for emergence and co-creation, my colleague and I were able to work with both planned and unplanned processes. We did not rely on the planning we had done in advance of the retreat to get us through; instead, we drew from our lived knowledge to course-correct and give the organization the opportunity to go deeper when they were ready.

PAUSING FOR POWER CHECKING AND
NAMING WHITE PRIVILEGE

One very important part of centering participation is to engage in process checks. It can be such a scary moment for facilitators. It forces one to get meta while in the middle of a process, to reveal the tools and processes we use and share that we don't quite know what to do next. And it's so badly needed. Not only does it give groups a chance to shift a meeting and get exactly what they need and deserve, it models the critical skills of working with uncertainty and emergence.

Some years ago, I was working with a small community activist group focused on supporting immigrants in their neighborhood. As far as I was concerned, things were going well. We had developed agreements for how we wanted to work together and were trucking along with the day's agenda of planning their work going forward.

Around midday, right before we were going to take a break, a participant, a person of color, said to me while we were still meeting as a group, "Hey, stop! This is not working for me. I do not like your facilitation." Then she ran off during the break. I went on a short walk around the block to clear my head and breathe through my mounting discomfort.

Part of me wanted to hide and run away, part of me just wanted to barrel through the day's agenda, and part of me wanted to know what was going on and address her concerns. I had inklings but didn't know for sure. I thought there might be power dynamics at play, given that she was a person of color and I am white.

During my short walk, I realized I had two choices: 1) I could facilitate the agenda as planned, or 2) I could take a process check and ask the participant what was going on for her. I decided to go with the process check. I needed to find out why my facilitation wasn't working for her and ascertain if this was the case for others in the group. After the break, I could either take her aside individually and ask her what was going on or I could talk with her as the group witnessed. I decided on the latter approach, as I thought it was important to acknowledge to everyone that a rupture had happened to the group's process and to learn together what was going on.

When we gathered after the break, the participant told me I had mispronounced her name multiple times and had asked only her for clarification of her ideas and not from white participants. I thanked her for sharing and raising my awareness, apologized for my mistreatment of her, owned that my white privilege had contributed to my treating her inequitably, promised her I would try to maintain an awareness and change my behavior, and invited all of the participants to please let me know if I continued to do anything that felt inequitable.

The process break cleared the air enough that we could keep working together, but I was nervous about how the day would proceed. At the end of the day, I did a check-in to see how people were doing. Much to my surprise, the woman who had shared her concerns told the group, with bright, happy eyes, that she was very grateful for the day, felt positive about the work we had accomplished together, and thought I was a great facilitator. What a turnaround!

It can seem very simple to take a moment out of a meeting to ask what is going on with an individual, but it takes skill and courage to do it in a way that balances the needs of an individual and the whole group. It also takes self-regulation when the process check is focused on one's own facilitation approach. I am forever learning, over and over again, that it is better to deal with some discomfort in a moment than give it time to fester. It saves a fair bit of grief on everyone's part.

FACILITATION GONE WRONG: RESISTING MEETING PARTICIPANTS' NEEDS

A few years ago, I was invited to attend a week-long retreat focused on developing storytelling skills. The workshop leader was a white man known for spinning homey tales from his childhood in the south. We were a mixed group of participants, with several people of color, queer people, young people, and social activist folks.

Each day, the workshop leader would teach a little lesson about how to tell a story well, and then we would spend much of our time together in small groups sharing very personal stories, often about loss and trauma, before coming back together as the full group, where a few of the stories were shared with everyone. On the second or third day of the workshop, when we gathered back together, a white male participant shared a story about his racist grandfather. Next, a Black woman spoke up and said, "We just told some very deep stories, and I'm wondering how they're sitting for those who shared and for those who received them." She wanted to know what the effect was on the white storyteller of telling his story and to discuss, as well, how it impacted us listeners, especially people of color.

The workshop leader interpreted this woman's comment as interrupting his workshop, and he attempted to steer the group back to a continued sharing of stories. Another participant then spoke up, saying, "Hey, we never generated working agreements in this group. I'm wondering about confidentiality." The workshop leader then responded that he had just presumed everyone would keep confidentiality, and as his words slipped out of his mouth, a collective unease in the room surfaced. Other participants chimed in, emphatically, explaining that we had not established any agreements for how we would be working together.

Throughout the week, the leader resisted our need to have discussions about the effects of telling stories in a mixed-race group that were about race and white privilege and trauma. He refused to engage in activities that would help us work together, including establishing agreements and checking in and out at the beginning and end of each day.

Our remaining time together predictably devolved into people of color separating themselves from the rest of the group for sanity, white people sharing with other white people how white privilege was affecting what was going on, and everyone squabbling with our leader, who kept complaining that we were derailing his teaching process.

Many of us were trying to say to him, in various ways, over and over again, "This is what our group needs right now, and this is an opportunity for you to be with us and learn about how you might change your workshops for the future." We tried lots of things to help show him what we needed. At one point, I stood up, approached the leader's flipchart, and used his own model of how a story is built to try to show him that we, collectively, were building a story together over these days, one that involved a beginning, a challenge, and perhaps a resolution. In that moment, he softened a bit, but not much changed.

The leader's resistance to shifting from his plan, refusal to engage in process checks, discomfort in sitting with the uncertainty of knowing where the group was going together, and resistance to the group taking up responsibility for their learning journey resulted in a hard, exhausting week. I can hardly remember anything I learned about storytelling, but I can clearly recall how poorly the space was held for us.

Our leader's approach reminded me of my undergrad theater professors depending on boring, staid living-room dramas in their teaching and direction. Orthodox Organizational Work, Orthodox Theater's equivalent in the world of organizational work, not Organizational Performance Art, Environmental Theater's equivalent, was dictating the underlying assumptions for how we would interact with each other. There was no room for joy, emergence, possibility, and certainly no space for thriving and liberation. We were locked in unresolved conflict about the underlying social constructs of our gathering and whether they were mutable.

Next, I delve into the relationship between embracing social constructionist theory and moving toward social justice and equity.

SOCIAL
CONSTRUCTIONISM

I HAVE BEEN DREAMING OF ANOTHER, BETTER WORLD FOR AS long as I can remember. When I am in despair regarding the many social, economic, and environmental inequities facing humanity and the earth, social constructionist theory is a guiding star, a propelling and underlying worldview in my practice of Organizational Performance Art, reminding me that many of our current realities are built on unspoken, taken for granted, and collectively held principles that can be unveiled, examined, toppled, and replaced. Social constructionist theory helps me believe that profound social change is possible. Here is Wikipedia's definition:

> Social constructionism is a theory of knowledge in sociology and communication theory that examines the development of jointly constructed understandings of the world that form the basis for shared assumptions about reality.[16]

I love Wikipedia's definition of social constructionism, Wikipedia itself being a "jointly constructed understanding of the world." It's nicely circular, self-referential, social.

Social constructionist theory laughs at the "shoulds" of humans, decenters taken-for-granted unspoken social agreements, and puts language to the distaste I have had since childhood for the many social fictions our world is organized upon. Money, authoritarian religion, gender, and two-party politics are a few of the social constructions that our society centers itself on that privilege white, male, able-bodied,

Christian, and heterosexual people. When I meditate on how many of
the foundations of our troubled, inequitable society are not real, but
social constructs, it's easier to imagine toppling them and replacing
them with something else, something much better.

I came out of the womb a social constructionist. As a small child, I
was not unique in thinking that all the world was a stage. I imagined the
whole world was playacting for me and was in service to my beingness. I
knew it was a fantasy, and it was not much of a leap to go from envision-
ing that everyone was playacting around me to understanding social
constructs. If I didn't like or agree with one of my parent's injunctions,
for example, I knew it was human made, and if human made it could be
human changed. I hardly ever accepted a "no" without fighting it. "No"
always felt like "maybe" or "it's possible." I remember nodding my head
and pretending to accept a "no" and going off and doing what I wanted.

Social constructionist theory informs how I work with groups. As
an outsider to the organizations and communities I work with, I can
more easily see how the ways people are behaving and interacting are
informed by their organizational culture, a jointly constructed understanding of how to be in a particular setting. Often I come in and ask
questions that might seem, upon first hearing them, stupid or naïve:
Tell me about what happens when a visitor arrives in your space. What
is the purpose of your weekly team meetings? How do you know when
a decision has been made? These kinds of questions invite folks to
describe their world, to become aware of what it looks like to new eyes,

to explain taken-for-granted ways of being, and to consider changing them. Organizational development scholar and consultant Frank Barrett writes, "From a social constructionist view, changing a system is a matter of changing a conversation."[17]

Of course, it is also very frightening and threatening to collectively peel back layers and talk about how the organizational sausage is being made. It can get ugly. Creating the conditions to build sufficient muscle for people to speak and hear the truths of what is going on is at the forefront of Organizational Performance Art. Some years ago, I supported a foundation as they undertook the journey to transform their internal organizational culture, build capacity, and develop strategy that aligned with their new, anti-racist mission focused on equity in education. This work was exciting, scary, edgy, righteous, full of possibility, and just. As a white woman consulting with a black-led, multi-racial organization, I most definitely did not hold all the keys that yielded change and growth, and many of the change processes were collaboratively designed and facilitated with people of color, both external consultants and internal staff.

The work with the foundation had three phases: Transitioning, Experimenting, and Re(de)fining. The Transitioning phase focused on staff developing, practicing, and reflecting on new ways of working together. We created new norms; examined past, current, and desired organizational cultures; articulated individual roles; designed new organizational models that depicted both direct reports and—equally important—how folks wanted to work together; and conceptualized how to operationalize the foundation's mission. We spent a lot of time during the Transitioning phase surfacing "ghosts," people who no longer worked there but who still haunted and influenced the foundation's culture in ways that manifested inequities.

The Experimenting phase involved supporting staff to develop the capacity, anchored in deep personal sharing, to work collaboratively to design and implement projects in support of a first year of grantmaking under their new mission. We also engaged in deep learning and practice regarding systemic racism and white privilege, and we began to exorcise their culture's inequitable "ghosts."

The Re(de)fining phase involved board development as well as continued work with staff. The board examined and changed their internal culture and practices to be more fully in alignment with the new mission, and the board and staff together developed a shared understanding of racial equity, crafting a theory of change around how to achieve equity in education.

The third phase heralded back to the first one, the Transitioning phase, as we practiced feedback loops, with continual check-ins with each other and the foundation's stated values, to determine how work was progressing and to assure there were the reflection and clarity needed for effective internal as well as external work with key stakeholders, notably grantees.

Raising awareness of and discussing with folks their taken-for-granted ways of being can produce a collective, giddy relief. Fostering such moments of delight focused on building equitable organizational culture is at the heart of Organizational Performance Art. As people are invited to examine and change their organization's social constructions, I often hear comments like: "We have permission to talk about *that*?", "We're finally talking about the elephant in the room!", and "Whew, now we're all acknowledging the emperor has no clothes."

CULTIVATING JOY AND SHARING DELIGHT

Poet and essayist Ross Gay writes that delight is the alchemical product of experiencing joy, coupled with the self-awareness and sharing of that experience.[18] Joy is the experience. Delight is the noticing, naming, and pointing out the joyful experience to others. In its job to name and notice, delight operates in a similar way as social constructionist theory, and it similarly centers joy and possibility.

One night a few years ago, Andrew, Egg, our niece, and I showed up at a theater to see a play, only to discover that our tickets were for the following week. I pouted and wheedled with the box office, trying to get us in, to no avail. Meanwhile, Andrew made the most delicious, sparkling drink out of our lemons, suggesting we go home and entertain each other with our own original, creative work. Andrew drummed, our niece read her poetry, Egg performed an improvised monologue, and I gave my very first reading of this (now reworked) essay on social constructionist theory. We had a rich, sweet evening together, and we marveled at, delighted in, the alchemy that yielded a more entertaining, joyful, and interactive evening than what awaited us down the other, unattainable path.

But how did we get to that experience of delight? How was I able to move from petulant, thwarted theater-goer to game joy-maker with my small group? It was Andrew's doing, of course. He knew we wouldn't be able to go to the theater that night, but we could make our own fun.

Andrew is clear about the things he can and cannot change. He self-identifies as a Stoic, embodying a philosophy articulated by the ancient Greeks. I have a slim book of writings, *The Art of Living*,[19] by Epictetus, a great Stoic writer from the first century AD, that Andrew shared with me years ago and that I have never fully read. Occasionally I'll flip it open, read a line or two, say "no thank you" and keep on whining about all the things affecting me that I cannot change. I come from a long line of hedonists, epicureans, pleasure-seekers, and Jewish complainers, and Stoicism does not come naturally to me. We make a good pair.

It was Andrew's ability to clearly see that there was no joy to be juiced that evening at the theater and his offer to find an alternative way for us to have fun together that allowed shared delight to enter our evening. Andrew's Stoic understanding of what he could and couldn't change about our situation allowed for that to happen.

Regardless of how Stoic I may or may not be, I know that fostering moments of communal thriving and liberation—fostering joy—and changing our reality based on social constructs—sharing delight—are central to the practice of Organizational Performance Art. Applying social constructionist theory offers us unlimited possibilities of social transformation in the service of justice and equity.

A social constructionist lens, however, is not welcome in all settings. Social constructionist theory is built on an understanding that many of our collectively created and held beliefs and practices are, at root, performative and mutable. Taking a peek and talking about what's happening behind a curtain are not always welcome. I will share a story here to illustrate.

POSSIBILITY LANGUISHING

In 2013, I participated in an experiential conference on group dynamics and processes hosted by the AK Rice Institute for the Study of Social Systems[20] and the Center for the Study of Groups and Social Systems.[21] The Group Relations conference methodology was developed in the 1960s under the guidance of Wilford Bion, president of the British Psychoanalytical Society. The guiding framework for interpreting group interactions leans heavily on psychoanalytic theories of behavior.

The conference I participated in involved a group of ten people (the "consultants") designing and holding a five-day meeting structure for forty other people (the "members") to explore their individual and group processes. During multiple group sessions, we explored our own projections and fantasies, trying to surface what was going on at unconscious levels, individually and collectively.

Much of our learning centered on noticing the largely unconscious roles we took up within our sessions, such as martyrs, scapegoats, kings, and queens. These roles were ones we naturally gravitated to and/or ones that a group projected onto us, representing the group's collective needs. Taking up a symbolic role is a two-way street. I have responsibility over my actions, and the group unconsciously assigns and interacts with archetypes projected onto me.

The Group Relations consultants took up tightly bounded roles that they did not budge from. They kept bounds with regard to time, task, and space in a manner that was orthodox and unyielding, similar to the differences in practice between Orthodox Theater and Environmental Theater. The consultants repeatedly redirected members to their task at hand, a frustratingly opaque directive to use the present moment with each other to learn about ourselves as individuals and as a group. They physically arranged meeting spaces in specific ways, often symbolically maintaining the hierarchy and separation of their role. When a meeting session was over, they stood up from their chairs and exited a room, without warning or salutation.

When putting on a traditional orthodox play, performers generally acknowledge that they are performing a character that is not themselves, and there are clear expectations for how audience members should behave, but when I showed up at the conference, this was not the case with the taciturn consultants seated in a line facing us. The consultants did not acknowledge their roles as ones they were performing or the activity we were engaging in together as performance. They said very little, and the purpose and bounds of the container they were holding were not clear to me. Was I to behave as an audience member attending a traditional orthodox play, or was this experience more like Environmental Theater, with no fourth wall and the freedom to interact however I'd like with the consultants/performers?

I experimented with the latter assumption. At the opening moments of the conference, I stood up, walked around, and asked questions about the unarticulated rules and roles of the gathering. Why are a few people, the consultants, sitting in a row facing several rows of many others, the members? Why are we all sitting instead of using our bodies in other ways? Why, why, why? I was largely met with silence.

During our morning-to-evening routine of back-to-back sessions, I found that I could not keep my body still. While most participants seemed content to sit, I stood up, walked, stretched, and sat on the floor. I also talked about what I was doing, that I was challenging unspoken norms around what was acceptable group behavior. While some members felt threatened by my moving around ("It's only 90 minutes. Can't you sit still for 90 minutes?"), others joined in with me.

One moment in particular stands out for me. Early in the conference, we were meeting as a full group. One person was missing, and perhaps it is not altogether surprising that in the pressure cooker of a psychologically intense, trying-to-perform-well-but-missing-a-player situation, embedded within the larger social context of a gun-friendly United States with frequent mass shootings, that we collectively drifted toward annihilation fantasies. It was shocking how quickly this happened. People shared improbabilities: "What if the missing person is dead?" "What if he barges through the doors right now and kills us?" What if, what if, what if? The tension was palpable. One participant woefully intoned, "We can't change the tone of this meeting."

"Oh yeah?" I cried out. "I can change it!" I shot out of my seat and started dancing, waving my hands, and chanting, "Dance, dance, dance with me!" While a few people joined in with clapping, everyone remained glued to their seats. I plopped back down, a spent tornado. The dreary conversation continued, tone unchanged. This was the lowest moment of the conference for me: sitting within a group collectively incapable of changing our morose tone, our social construct of joylessness and stuckness.

While some people told me that they admired my verve, I remember also feeling out of control. I had gone too far in freely expressing myself, and I felt like a cartoon. I was working too hard, consciously and unconsciously, to meet the group's need for communal thriving, and at the same time limiting my ability to take up leadership that would be truly valued.

Toward the end of the conference, each participant received an individual consultation, witnessed by a few members. We each reflected on our participation and consultants shared their observations of each of us. Consultants ascribed to members roles we were performing within the group. I was told I was taking up a role of the edgewalker, someone who cannot acquiesce to the given culture or strictures of a situation. My consultant's words still haunt me: "Who would want to work with someone that always wants to burn down the house?"

After the conference, I worried that my house-burning tendencies needed to be tamed, that my social constructivist stance toward human institutions and practices would alienate organizations I wanted to work with. But there's another way to dance with this fun house mirror of the conference. From the consultants' point of view, I was being a rebel, wanting to break every rule. But that presumes that the rules of the game—the rules for members—had been implicitly or explicitly articulated. I don't believe they were. Or if they were, I am not confident that I was sufficiently aware of them.

From an opposite point of view, I was embodying expansion, creativity, openness, invitation, critical thinking, playfulness, experimentation, and full participation. I was more like a Bread and Puppet flag runner inviting in joy or a puppeteer playing with possibility, and I was shocked and saddened to have my contribution not well received.

My experience at the Group Relations conference was not unlike that of four audience members Richard Schechner wrote about in *Environmental Theater* who came to see The Performance Group's *Dionysus in 69*.[22] The performance had two rules for audience members. They were: 1) you do not have to participate, and 2) when invited to participate, you can designate someone else in your stead. The performance came to a halt when the four chose not to participate and also to not designate someone else. From Schechner's perspective, the four declined to participate in a way expected of them by the performers; however, the four felt they did follow the rules, as their interpretation of the first rule was that designating someone else was participation, which they had decided not to do. Schechner described the four audience members as square refuseniks, possibly litigious, drunk with their petty power to stop the performance. But I am left wondering: perhaps the four were practicing social constructionist theory, exercising their sense of curiosity and possibility. Maybe they wanted to see what might happen next if they fully refused to participate.

I am also left wondering about the design choices of the Group Relations conference and how they were a reflection of its underlying social constructions, its underlying culture. I am especially concerned with how dominant white culture was seemingly valued at the Group Relations conference. Dominant white culture, or white supremacy culture, is comprised of cultural practices and beliefs that have histori-cally allowed white ruling class people to apply what Tema Okun calls "the pseudo-scientific concept of race to create whiteness and a hierarchy of racialized value."[23]

In particular, the exclusive reliance on psychoanalysis for interpretation of individual and group behavior at the Group Relations conference reflects white supremacy cultural characteristics of paternalism and a belief that there is only one right way to interpret things. Other elements of white supremacy culture, such as power hoarding and binary either/or thinking, parallel the choice to utilize two groups—consultants and members—that are constructed to be at odds with each other. I am concerned that these design choices, these social constructs, limited members' ability to form a community centered on joy and possibility, and I wonder how different guidelines, different social constructs, could have yielded greater thriving and liberation.

TRANSFORMING WHITE SUPREMACY ORGANIZATIONAL CULTURE

My lifelong dance with social constructionist theory helps me see and critique many taken-for-granted organizational practices. It has informed my choice to keep to the peripheries of organizations, supporting them in their development, and not joining in as a full member. Organizational consultants can dip in and out of different worlds to creatively support groups in developing new ways of being together. As people who hop from group to group—country to country, really—consultants can easily identify the rules—social constructs—that are tied to specific, generally unarticulated values. We can see how particular practices help or hinder people in showing up as their authentic selves and working well together.

One of my core drives in practicing Organizational Performance Art is to help transform with and for others the oppressions that come from enduring competitive, hierarchical work environments based on white supremacy cultural values. The many practices used to control staff, such as requiring approval for vacation time or having to meet productivity measures, go back much farther in time than what most organizational scholars usually attribute these practices to: the rise of factory work during the industrial age and the development of "scientific management" of repetitive, meaningless labor that replaced cottage industries with their more engaging, autonomous models of work. There are earlier, more pernicious influences on today's work environments, notably the practices used by white people to maintain control on plantations over enslaved people of African descent.[24]

I help support the development of the conditions needed for communal thriving and liberation. Much of the work I do in culture transformation is helping groups to understand how white supremacy culture shows up in their workplaces and developing different ways of being together that can counter it. It can start with questions that reveal the taken-for-granted ways of doing things: Why do you do it this way and not that way? How did it come to be this way? What does it feel like for you to be here? How about for folks with different social identities than yours? What does this place look like for folks who are just walking through the door for the first time? Then we can talk about what needs to change and develop new practices.

Developing an understanding that many workplace practices are built on social constructs with foundations in white supremacy culture does not mean change can immediately happen, however. Like my response to the theater that couldn't give our little group seats to a sold-out performance, staff sometimes bump their heads against what feels like an implacable organizational construct. Unlike the solution Andrew offered to our group—let's make our own joy—people working in organizations founded on the values of white supremacy culture may find they can go only so far to create new possibilities from within. I have often heard from people who want to be change-makers that they are not authorized to do so. I also have heard from leaders who say they are not allowed to give authority to other folks, especially those whom they supervise.

This stuckness of working within hierarchies of authority is frustrating all around; it affects people at all organizational "levels." While power inequities within hierarchies may be named, it is much more difficult to change them. Organizations can move toward communal liberation and thriving only as far as their decision makers are willing to go. This is meeting the hard edges of social constructionist theory. Just because one sees that a workplace is a constructed reality, even one based on white supremacy culture, does not mean one can easily change it.

I wish I could end this chapter on a much more upbeat note, but I am at a loss. The practice of social constructionist theory and Organizational Performance Art has its limits and is not a panacea, of course, to the social injustices and inequities residing within many organizations, communities, and the world at large. I believe that less hierarchical structures, such as worker-owned cooperatives, where collective decision-making and ownership are fundamental, offer a model that will get us closer to communal thriving and liberation; however, it is a long slog to build a more equitable and just world. In the next chapter, I discuss how the use of physical space, regardless of organizational structure and values, can catalyze more liberating ways of being together. It's time to move on to examining an organizational element, space, that we can more easily control.

SPACE SENSE

AS A TEENAGER I SPENT MANY HOURS WANDERING THROUGH physical spaces, developing and tuning myself as an instrument of awareness. I remember the weird explorations by foot and bike that I took all over Forest Park in St. Louis. There was a fall day where I entered the backstage of the outdoor Muny Theater in the park. The summer's run of musicals and concerts had passed, and somehow the place had not been secured. I slipped in and wandered about the inner temple of props and sets, feeling the charge of their performative possibilities.

I continue to go on weird walks. Now, I often go on journeys to the sea. On the first anniversary of my Mom's death, her yahrzeit, I spent the day with Ash. It was also Simchat Torah, the Jewish holiday that celebrates completing the annual cycle of reading the Torah, the five books of Moses. Simchat Torah is traditionally celebrated with dancing in the street with Torahs and flags. Ash and I danced to celebrate her grandmother, my mother. Instead of a Torah, I clutched the last book of stories my Mom wrote. Next, we hopped a ferry and crossed the waters and boroughs to arrive at the sea, our original mother, where we happened upon flowers and fruit scattered along her shores. We built an altar with shells, a cantaloupe, oranges, and flowers. Ash inscribed the sand with the Hebrew letters yud-hay-vav-hay, the invocation of is-was-will-be. We danced, we meditated, we breathed deeply, we remembered.

Organizational Performance Art applies a deep, visceral sensitivity for how a physical environment affects individual and group process. It looks for ways to make a space more inviting to expansive conversation and change. Blinds can be drawn to reveal sunshine and the world beyond. Tables can be moved or set aside. Chairs can be arranged and rearranged—first a circle, now dyads, now small groups. Or they can be ditched entirely. Is there space for people who want to stand, perhaps stretch, instead of sit? Is the floor clean and warm? Some folks may want to sit or lie on it. The surface of the walls should not be precious; we need to post giant sheets of paper to record our ideas. The lighting should not be harsh; maybe we'll even turn it off and rely on natural light. How is the temperature? We don't want to wear sweaters in the middle of the summer, or peel down to our tank tops in the winter. Are there rooms or corners we can retreat to for quiet or small group work? Is there access to the outdoors for breaks? Perhaps we'll even take our work together outside.

I have consulted in many different physical spaces, and the ones I have found most conducive to supporting the conditions for communal thriving and liberation are the ones that allow for the greatest freedoms in arranging bodies in interaction with space. Of course, one doesn't always have as much control over the physical environment as one would like. Too often there is a vast conference table—solid, dominating, and unmovable—taking up too much space in the middle of a windowless room. Wires spill out of holes in the middle of the table's huge plane; giant wall-mounted screens monitor the space with their large, grey, unblinking eyes; and strange, antiquated-looking speaker phones plant themselves, like giant bugs, in the corners of the room. Walls are covered with nicely framed corporate art, and tall, padded chairs encircle the table, all facing forward, toward a solitary seat at the end.

When I encounter such mammoth, formal rooms with their presumptions of top-down engagement, I take a corner and circle up a few of the giant chairs, cover the corporate art with flip chart paper, turn off the florescent overhead lights, hide the speaker phone, and cover a door's window for privacy. Then we can get to work in a way that is more welcoming, inclusive, and equitable, in a way that allows for more joy and possibility.

I lead an organizational culture activity where staff walk around and try to see with new eyes their physical environment, notice what it feels like, using all their senses. I ask folks: What does that poster on the wall look like to someone who is coming to this space for the first time? Who is the first person you see, and what kind of interaction do you have when you first enter? What do you see? What do you hear? What do you feel? What do you hunger for?

You can learn a great deal about an organization's culture just by walking through their space. Sometimes the space is too divided up by shelving and files and walls and doors. It is labyrinthine and there is no natural flow. Folks who should be working together are scattered at different ends of a floor. Other times there just isn't enough privacy for people to feel they can collect their own thoughts, have some autonomy. Desks are smushed right up against other desks. Over time, casual lounge and meeting spaces meant for socializing and restoration become storage units, with piles of boxes precariously teetering in the corners, near abandoned, broken chairs.

I once consulted for an organization where I initially assumed the first person I saw, sitting behind a desk facing the entry, had a role of

welcoming people as they entered the space. In fact, this was not the case. They were program staff, and it made for a confusing and awkward introduction to this person and their organization. I learned, not surprisingly, that their physical placement in the office disrupted their work, as they felt compelled to greet and orient each new person as they arrived. So much time and energy was being spent on needless, confusing interactions rather than ones that would serve both parties and the organization's mission.

Another time, I worked with a social service organization that had separate entrances for clients and staff. The client entrance was unkempt and at the back of the building, conveying that the people the organization served, folks who were disproportionately people of color and those with economic disadvantage, were not fully welcome. The arrangement felt like it was maintaining an inequitable status quo. It conveyed that nothing of real significance was going to change for people who entered this space.

On a more promising note, I once worked with an organization that decided to undertake a massive redesign of their board room to allow for greater flexibility and connectivity. They jettisoned the ponderous, immovable table that kept everyone away from each other and replaced it with multiple, smaller ones that could easily be configured in any number of ways. Their social equity values showed up both in how they used space and in their richer, more liberating ideas that came from meetings using space more flexibly.

I was trucking along, supporting organizations in using their space creatively and equitably, when the COVID-19 pandemic hit. Group process work, like much work in general, pivoted to being conducted in virtual space. Overnight, my physical workspace narrowed down to my small little office, a monk-like cell, where I Zoomed out to the world with other people in their own little cells. Questions I asked folks about how their organizational spaces impacted their work and relationships were no longer relevant, and the electric connection of working with people in real space was gone.

Facilitating meetings on Zoom did not feel like Organizational Performance Art. What once felt energizing and replenishing now left me feeling drained, disembodied, and disconnected. Presence was harder to maintain and for others to pick up on in the Zoom world. My facial expressions became over-animated while the rest of my body remained immobile, facing one direction.

During the first month of the pandemic, I went on a walk through Brooklyn's Prospect Park—a vast space—with a friend, a six-foot-long measuring stick held between us. Part absurdist performance, part public expression of despair, we wandered about, taking pictures of ourselves and raising peoples' eyebrows. How could we work well together when we had to be so far apart? I wrote a newsletter wondering what might be the invitation in not being able to share space together. Below is an excerpt:

What is the invitation for how to use space in this moment?

My city—and the world at large—is addicted to busy-ness. Business is busy-ness. Rush, rush, rush. Now, there is nowhere to rush. Yet there is a frantic energy to get everyone to work together online. The internet has become our savior. It makes us feel productive, connected, "normal."

But the internet is not our savior. These are not "normal" times. And I don't know why we are collectively in such a rush to get back to the same ol' activities that feed capitalism and inequality.

Here are some invitations for how to use space right now:

Being alone is good. I often prefer to be alone, in the quiet, to gazing at the faces of my colleagues on a screen.

Stay in your body. Zoom calls feel disembodied. I'm wishing for more phone calls where we quietly listen and meaningfully respond, where we can feel ourselves sitting on our couches or floors or chairs, our feet on the earth, breathing.

Go outdoors. Be part of a larger world. The fresh air, the sounds, the smells. I feel this as much when I take out the trash as when I walk in the park. Just standing on the stoop gives me a new vista.

Connect with real people when you can. Hang out on your stoop or front entrance and say "hi" to neighbors as they pass. A few days ago, my family drummed outside our house; children from across the street joined in on their stoop.

Remember that we are energetically connected. There are so many people I want to be in space with right now: friends, families, clients, colleagues. I am trusting that we are holding each other in our hearts and following our intuition for when it will be the right time to physically connect.

Deprived of my previously taken-for-granted opportunities for novel, symbiotic renewal with humans, I took to communing with trees. One morning, I kicked off my shoes, plopped down in the dew-kissed grass and meditated for a bit. I then stuffed in my earbuds, stashed my phone in my fanny pack, pressed "shuffle" on my "Alissa's good stuff" playlist, and let the magic happen.

The music poured straight into my body, a flowing, golden elixir. I danced, marched, sang, stretched, flexed, rond de jambed, rolled, jumped, shook, skipped, and breathed. With the trees, with the sky, with the sun, with the earth. When I had sweated it all out and felt done, I looked at the trees again, and these words came to me:

The trees move way more than we do.
Only our hair waves in the wind,
but all their branches and leaves
flutter and sway with every breath,
like flags.

They may pity us for our inability
to dance and flutter with the present,
our somnambulant hubris in believing that
our incessant chatter and activity
is superior.

I had never considered before how trees may be freer than us humans, but in that moment I could see how all their parts were able to move and bend as conditions around them changed. I was frustrated at how unbending we humans seemed in comparison. We Zoomed and Zoomed and Zoomed all day, keeping ourselves still and contained, protecting ourselves and each other. We never stopped and took a breath and wondered if we needed all this chatter.

After a few more months of Zooming, I badly needed to roam more freely in space, to feel joy and possibility for humanity, to glimpse a way toward communal thriving and liberation. Turning even more deeply inward, I learned about shamanic practice. When the practice of Organizational Performance Art was less accessible, shamanic practice opened up cavernous spaces of social change in my spirit and imagination.

SHAMANIC

PRACTICE

DURING THOSE FIRST FEW MONTHS OF THE PANDEMIC WHEN people were learning how to navigate space differently, I began to learn about and practice shamanic journeying. It gave me a meaningful, accessible practice that was uncompromised by the social isolation strictures that made Organizational Performance Art difficult to practice. Shamanic practice was a calling I was finally heeding after many years of wondering about it, a question I had coiled deep inside me that I had largely ignored.

The word "shaman" felt too charged for me to explore, evoking mystical ways of knowing and seeing that were dismissed in my upbringing. A professor in mathematics, my Dad prized abstract thinking and logic. He subscribed to a journal called *The Skeptical Inquirer*. I remember the black and white images of bizarre phenomena—ghosts and UFOs and spoon-bending—and I remember the research to disprove them using the scientific method. The most recent issue of *The Skeptical Inquirer* was always proudly arrayed on our magazine rack, alongside copies of *Science* and *Scientific American*.

One day I was telling Ash, who shares with me a yearning for exploring the mystical and the unseen in our everyday reality, about my Dad's antipathy for the mystical. I told her about my Dad's beloved *Skeptical Inquirer* and, for the first time, I thought, "Methinks he doth protest too much." Why was it so important that my Dad subscribe and proudly display this rag that derided the unknown? Perhaps my Dad was keeping close by what was fascinating to him but did not fit his world-view. The unknown was in a box, locked up with empirical logic.

Is it so utterly anathema to muse over the prospect of my Dad being a closet mystic? Antonin Artaud, avant-garde actor and theater director from the early 20th century, writes about the difference between a traditional actor's use of pretense and a committed performer's embodiment of authenticity:

> If there is still one hellish, truly accursed thing in our time, it is
> our artistic dallying with forms, instead of being like victims
> burnt at the stake, signaling through the flames.[25]

Perhaps my Dad was closeted even to himself, "dallying with the forms" of the unknown, subscribing to *The Skeptical Inquirer,* but "signaling through the flames" to his daughter that the unknown, the mystical, is worthy of exploration. I think my Dad's mathematical exploration—the search for new theories to prove—was a vast exploration of the unknown. His embrace of only one path to knowledge, the scientific method, seems uncharacteristically dogmatic.

In the middle of the pandemic, hungering for novelty, depth, and connection, shamanic practice was an obvious attractor to me. Fortunately, my friend Helen Klonaris was offering an online beginner's workshop in shamanic journeying called *We Are All Made of Stars.*[26] I knew Helen from when we were in college together; she was a performer in

Made in the CFA. Helen had been all set to launch an in-person wisdom school, and then the pandemic interrupted her plans. She courageously pivoted to the world of online offerings.

In addition to offending my skeptical ancestors, I was hesitant to learn about shamanism because of my concerns of cultural appropriation of its practices by white people; however, I learned from Helen that shamanic practice is in the cultural DNA of many peoples, including white Europeans, and accessing it is a universal human birthright. I also learned from Richard Schechner's writing in *Environmental Theater* that the origins of many different practices, including theater, religious, and psychological work, branch from a common tree of shamanic practice.[27]

Shamanic practice has been around for at least 30,000 years and came from a time when humans lived in awe of nature, a time before we invented deities and made nature work with us, a time before agriculture and animal husbandry. The word shaman means "one who knows" and comes from the word "saman" from the Tungus tribe in Siberia. A shaman is one who can raise, or excite, their energy and shift into non-ordinary consciousness.

Shamanic practice invites us to use our wisdom, imagination, and collective myths, symbols, and stories to directly access healing and insight for personal, ancestral, cultural, and social need. "Healing" can be a somewhat limiting term, often associated with something received by a helpless victim to rid themselves of a malady. A person heals from trauma, cancer, or abuse, but healing can be much more transformative than that. It is not just the getting rid of the bad but the infusion of the good. Using the term this way is akin to using the term "medicine" in an expansive way. Medicine addresses not only what ails; it can enrichen, enliven. Medicine includes good food and good works that support the body and the soul. Healing is the same. Healing enriches, enlivens. It supports our thriving and liberation.

Helen's ability to move beyond the obvious limitations of online technologies to guide us in deep, embodied practice and to connect with one another is worthy of an essay of its own. She seriously threw down, holding space, love, compassion, curiosity, and invitation, all with an anti-colonial, anti-racist stance.

Helen taught us that "the bridge to cross into the spirit realm is our own imagination" and gave us an easily accessible sequence of activities to help us enter a state conducive to journeying. The first step was to develop specific questions or intentions for a journey. This could be looking for a spirit guide or seeking wisdom or healing on a particular issue. Journaling on one's question or intention and locating where it dwells in one's body were also useful practices to engage in before going on an actual journey.

The next step was to engage in a physical practice to raise one's energy in support of entering a different state of consciousness. Helen instructed us to dance in our own physical spaces, video feed turned off, to trance-like music with a steady beat.

The next step was to begin the journey itself. I would lie on the floor of my little room, my eyes covered with a special hood I used for this purpose. Helen instructed us to first imagine we were entering a Middle World, which was a real place on earth, in "ordinary" reality that we knew well. It could be the room we were in, a place in nature, or anywhere else we wanted to begin. Designating the place as a Middle World allowed us to infuse it with magic, with spirit, with "nonordinary" reality.

A Middle World where I often began my journeys was the stage of Bread and Puppet Theater, both in the fields of Vermont and on the concrete floor of the theater they perform in when they come to New York City. In the Middle World, just as I had in real life, I ran flags or donned a mask or puppet, animating clouds, chairs, a buffalo, a red devil, or Mother Earth. I was part of, surrounded by, and making magic, spirit, joy, and possibility.

From the Middle World–made magic, we allowed our imaginations, our spirits, to travel to either a Lower or Upper World, where we would find, develop, discern, or dream beings, spirits, and images that responded to the question or intention of our journey. We spent time in these worlds learning, breathing, and communing. Next, we thanked spirits who had engaged with us and followed Helen's voice and drumming to guide us back to the Middle World. There, we gave ourselves time to transition from our altered states of consciousness back to being present in "ordinary" reality. We took time to write down what we had experienced and to rest, before resuming our doings back in "ordinary" reality.

During a time when it felt impossible to practice Organizational Performance Art, to work in person, in real space, in service to communal thriving and liberation, shamanic journeying opened and held expansive, imaginative, cavernous space within myself. It gave me a practice in exploring the possibilities of different worlds centered on social justice and equity.

As the pandemic continued, seemingly without end, I went on a series of journeys to understand the virus at its center. In one journey, I imagined that Coronavirus was feeling out of control and hadn't meant to run rampant:

> Poor Coronavirus. She wasn't meant to live in the air. She was
> only there because the earth was too sullied, trampled upon, to
> sustain her.

In another journey, I was looking for a spirit teacher, and Corona presented herself in the middle of a muddy meadow in Manhattan's Central Park. She showed me how worms turn the earth into something useful for others. They take waste and make it habitable. We humans have a lot to learn from worms. Corona then showed me the trees, the wise being with their roots in the ground, interacting with the worms, and their branches in the heavens, reaching out to heavenly ones. Corona was a microcosm of the spherical earth and her trees branching outward—two spiked globes reaching out and touching all.

> Do you see how hard other worlds are trying to fend off Earth,
> so we humans don't infect them? The more we stay close to the
> ground, the safer it is for other worlds.

I discerned that Coronavirus was guiding humans in the opportunity to heal ourselves and the earth, to undo what we have wrought with racism, colonialism, resource extraction, and hoarding, to make good, to transform ourselves and the planet back to a Middle World, an ordinary reality infused with good intention. Our job is to commune with our ancestors, stay close to the earth, become a "barefoot people" where humanity is decentered. When the earth heals, Coronavirus will return to it, where she belongs.

These journeys to seek spiritual understanding of and guidance from Corona helped me thrive during difficult times. They helped me accept the realities of social isolation and further contemplate the relationship between a global pandemic that was ravaging humanity, especially people of color and those with economic disadvantage, and the many ways we humans ravage the earth.

I also went on shamanic journeys to seek wisdom from nonordinary reality about humanity healing from racism and white supremacy culture. On one journey, shortly after the murder by police of George Floyd and the global protests it ignited, I began with the daunting and urgent question of what a world without racism would look like. I began my journey in a Middle World that was one of the locations for protests in Brooklyn, a few blocks from my home. There, in real life, chalk messages had been inscribed onto the road between the subway station and Prospect Park: Asian Jews For Black Lives. George Floyd. Breonna Taylor. Eric Garner. Ahmaud Arbery. Abner Louima. Black Lives Matter. And "Why does the color of my skin frighten you?"

During the journey, I stood among protestors, six feet apart, masked, fists in the air. There were no police. We were barefoot on the grass, where Corona had returned and would not harm us. There was no pavement, and the grass extended in all directions. I visited the Drummers Grove, an actual site in Prospect Park where Black people have gathered weekly since the 1960s to play drums, dance together, and be in community. In my journey, I saw a cargo net strung in the trees above the Drummers Grove. It was full of artifacts from a prior time that we were no longer part of. It was an anti-lynching memorial, with remnants of destroyed police cars and other artifacts from an oppressive regime. It had slowly decayed, faded, up in the air, a monument and reminder, but no longer of us.

> We are the Brooklyn Commune. There is no money. There are no clocks. There are no schools. There is peace and sharing and grass in all directions.

This journey gave me a healing social vision of possibility born from our current inequitable circumstances, but I was troubled about how to get to that place, the Brooklyn Commune. On a subsequent journey, I chose to focus on how to end dominant white culture's ways of hoarding capital. I began my journey in a Bread and Puppet Middle World, inhabiting a bison puppet with Ash, the same puppet we had performed with a few years prior, in real life. At that time, Ash and I were instructed to breathe together so that the bison would come alive for the audience. We held the wooden armature and slowly synchronized soft movements up and down to our paired breathing: two white people inhabiting a bison, an animal that was brought nearly to obliteration at the hands of white people many decades earlier. A fraught, complex image to begin this journey.

In the journey, I rode the bison through the celestial world, where money was meaningless. I travelled to a star, shining all directions through time, connecting past, present, and future. The star offered me light to bring back to the charging bull sculpture at Wall Street. The bison and I descended down, down, down back to Earth, landing at the bull, a bronze being raging with unbridled greed and power. The bull became infused with the light. It glowed from behind his eyes. The bull then shapeshifted into a bison, which became a field of bison, roaming all of Manhattan, across the Eastern Seaboard to the White House.

The museum across from the bull, the Smithsonian's Museum of the American Indian, crumbled down and rose up again as a new institution. The little white men in their pinstriped nightshirts who got in the way of the world returning to bison were put away there. As the bison roamed, all the money in the world fell back to the ground, decomposed and fertilized the earth, shooting back up as grass.

A year of solitude, dancing with trees, and shamanic journeying passed. Then another began. New questions emerged for me: What did it mean for humanity that we had not gathered together in person for over a year, that we had not yet returned to space? What were we not even aware of losing when we continued to meet in virtual space?

I knew what it felt like for me. I felt circumscribed by a quiet, invisible, impermeable bubble. My senses were drawn in, I was physically contained, and my interior world was enormous. It felt like I was holding space for joy and possibility for my interior world, the only space I could really hold.

While my learning from shamanic practice was getting richer and richer, my group process work on Zoom was becoming more and more stagnant. Sometimes I wasn't even sure how much I wished anymore to be in an actual, tangible room, guiding a group through deep process. These were the days when my colleague realized when she asked her client if everyone would be in the same room together for a meeting that she wasn't aware that she meant sharing virtual space together. She was aghast at how the pandemic had altered her imagination.

Maybe the pandemic had changed me too much. I had, by necessity, let go of my desire for in-person holding of space for joy and possibility, while watering the things I could accomplish within the confines of my little room. I hoped that in the near future, when people would be able to again physically gather, that my little withered arm holding my Organizational Performance Art wand would want to grow strong again, like a starfish, once cut, regenerating itself.

One day, I engaged in a particularly intense journey with an intention of exploring the relationship between acceptance and acquiescence. How could I discern the difference between an accepting of versus an acquiescing to circumstances I couldn't change, such as not being able to engage in in-person Organizational Performance Art and enduring the pandemic itself? After my journey, I wrote:

> The wind is acceptance. It always blows. Acquiescence is a deep, dark void, a stagnant mud puddle. It receives no wind. It is falling, falling, falling into the abyss, as opposed to seeing it, dancing with it, flying over and through and with it, using our wind to navigate it.

Acceptance seemed like an important survival—even thriving—mechanism that inspires different ways of coping with a challenge, while acquiescence seemed like admitting defeat and giving up. As I moved out of my journey and back into ordinary reality to get on with the rest of my day, my back violently spasmed, causing great pain, and forcing me to the floor. It was as if the teaching I had received was too much for the compromised state I had devolved to while enduring the pandemic. My Organizational Performance Art was in a state of acquiescent stagnation, and my body was loudly protesting.

Around the same time, I developed a painful, itchy skin condition that plagued me for three months, stumping doctors who prescribed to me, over time, a total of ten different medications. I learned, as well, from other friends about their own strange physical maladies that were not healing well. I began to wonder if our immune systems and abilities to heal ourselves were being compromised by the long-term stress of living under the strictures of COVID-19.

My friend Eleanor, with whom I was consulting regarding the direction of a community center she co-founded in rural New Hampshire, had a different take on my maladies, however. She thought I was shedding my skin, getting ready for my next iteration as healer and Organizational Performance Artist. She recounted a similar time in her life when her body rebelled against her, after giving birth to twins whom she had carried for friends who were not able to bear children:

After I had the twins and let them go, I had the worst back problems. I wasn't used to that. I had had three kids and I could go back to work the day after my children were born. The teacher I was working with said, "You had to prove to yourself the enormity of what you just went through." It was a pivotal axis shift in our life. "You need to figure out what your body is telling you."

Eleanor then made a connection to my own state:

I'm thinking of the death of your mom, then the pandemic. You're in an axis shift, and it's explosive for you.

It was time to accept, not acquiesce to, the strictures of the pandemic. It was time to recharge Organizational Performance Art.

COMING TO
OUR SENSES

TOGETHER
AGAIN

AFTER ENDURING MORE THAN A YEAR OF THE PANDEMIC, having had no opportunity for facilitating in-person meetings and exclusively using virtual meeting technologies, I began to think about how to address the sensory deprivation that people around the world were collectively enduring. I and everyone I was working, playing, and parenting with were fried from all the screen time, the disembodied numbness of turning our bodies in one direction, performing for a bunch of rectangles that sometimes revealed faces and sometimes did not. Perhaps it is not surprising that the sensory deprivation—taste and smell—that so many people were experiencing when they became ill with COVID-19 paralleled the sensory deprivation of meeting together virtually.

In my tiny pandemic office, I was tired of going on solo shamanic journeys, stilling my body, wandering around in my spirit and imagination in search of communal thriving and liberation. I hungered for deep, embodied communion with other people and sensed that others yearned for this, as well. I wanted a shared realness—smells and touch and taste—and I wondered what other people were feeling in their bodies, in their spaces. I fantasized about sniffing along the edges of my Zoom screen, reaching into the innards of my laptop and touching my fellow Zoomers. How would we be able to share senses again, experience together real joy and possibility?

In the spring of 2021, the morning after our second pandemic Passover seder on Zoom, I woke up dreaming for a *Seder of the Senses*, a collective, textless communion via our bodies. The traditional seder is layered and confusing, a mishmash of text and ritual, masked as order, celebrating our enslaved Jewish ancestors' freedom. Some things we point to on our table and never eat. Some things we read about being on our table but we actually don't have them there. Some people are talked about in our oral tradition, but don't show up in the actual text. This jumble masked as order is what it can feel like in organizational life, as well. I wanted a seder, an organizational gathering, centered on our af (nose), peh (mouth) or (skin), oznayim (ears), and ayin (eyes).

In my tiny pandemic office, the four walls protecting others from me and me from others, I began to imagine leading meetings centered on sensory activities. I called it a *Theater of the Senses*, with the intention of adapting embodied practices based on experimental theatrical and other somatic traditions for use with a wide array of people. I hungered to take people through exercises where they could commune and get past the sensory deprivation of a year of lockdown. Richard Schechner's description in *Environmental Theater* of leading performers through activities where they explored their physical space separately and together was an inspiration.[28] So were the athletic approaches Polish director Jerzy Grotowski used to get actors to ground their performances in physical impulses, which he described in *Towards a Poor Theatre*.[29] I also drew on the symbolic imagery work that I had adapted from Brazilian director Augusto Boal's techniques.[30]

With the use of COVID-19 vaccines, the world was slowly beginning to open up again, and I allowed myself to dream about doing work in a way that would enliven my and others' senses, that would address what we had endured from being physically isolated from each other. I wrote a newsletter titled *Coming to Our Senses, Together, Again*, which included these passages:

> As we enter our sixteenth month of COVID, how do we want to be together? I want to center the physical wonder of coming back together, the glee of sharing our senses, the mourning of the profound losses and deprivation we've endured, the mystery of feeling our bodies being in one place, together, again.
>
> Imagine an activity called Rooting Around:
>
> Go to a place with earth, fresh air, dirt, roots, grubs. Root around. Commune. Breathe. Share something you found, noticed, learned, spent time with. Don't use words. Share through your grunts, sniffs, gaze, movement.
>
> This does not mean, of course, that I imagine in the organizational gatherings I look forward to facilitating that we are rolling in the mud, but it does mean that I want us to take seriously the gift of being together, again, in the same space. What do we want to feel together? See together? Remember together?
>
> Coming to Our Senses, Together, Again. Let us gather in a field. Real or metaphorical. Come Close. Sniff. Root. Gallop. Cavort.
>
> Let us stay present to the wonder of our coming back together, again.

My dreaming felt preposterous. When would I ever actually have an opportunity to work this way? When would people start meeting together in person, much less in ways that centered our multiple senses and not just our talking heads? How would I identify and connect with an organization or community that wanted this kind of work?

At the beginning of the second year of the pandemic, my friend Eleanor reached out to me for individual coaching and organizational support. She was trying to figure out what was the next step on her journey from urban activist in the 1960s to socially conscious macrobiotic farmer in the 1970s to early childhood educational teacher and director since the 1980s. Eleanor lived on a rural land trust in New Hampshire that also housed the Orchard School and The Center at Orchard Hill, a place she had helped found, build, and run.

Year-round Orchard School programming operated for many years until interpersonal dynamics and precarious finances forced it to unceremoniously fizzle out a few years prior to the pandemic. When Eleanor contacted me, something else wanted to emerge, but she didn't know what that was or how to go about finding out. There was no clear, central, unifying sense of purpose held by a group of people.

Eleanor wanted to surround herself and the land with people who could support her in an emerging, yet unknown vision of service, community, and social justice. She put out a call to people who had been in deep relationship with The Center and the land over the years. She wrote, "We have the vaccine now and know how to minimize risk. The risk of losing connection and joy is a far greater concern."

I told Eleanor about my desire for a *Theater of the Senses,* and she imagined the possibilities for The Center immediately. We decided that I would come to their place at the end of the summer to facilitate a multi-day series of activities called, like the newsletter I had sent, *Coming to Our Senses, Together, Again.* Eleanor identified a core group of people to work with, and for the first time since the pandemic had stopped me in my tracks nearly eighteen months prior, I had the enormous pleasure of planning work that would be live, on land, with a group of people interested in working together toward communal thriving and liberation.

Over that summer, I developed a playbook for a *Theater of the Senses*. It had descriptions for multiple activities that focused on awakening, individually and collectively, the senses in four groupings:

- Space Sense (sight, kinesthetic)

- Sound Sense (listening, making sound)

- Visceral Sense (taste, smell, gut)

- Image/Symbolic Sense (imagination)

I chose these senses, as opposed to the five we generally conceptualize (seeing, hearing, tasting, touching, and smelling) because they more comprehensively tap into the many ways of sensing the world and each other that people had collectively been deprived of during the pandemic.

From the playbook, I chose activities that would serve our time together, and headed to New Hampshire for a week. It was a blissful, dreamy week. Almost all of our work was done outdoors, on the land. When we first came together, we created a space in the center to invoke people and spirits not physically with us whose energy we wanted to include and pay tribute to. As we placed rocks in the center, we named our children, our grandparents, the land, mentors, and many creatures and spirits.

Later, I instructed each person to spend some time alone, reflecting on their relationship with The Center and the land, with particular attention to moments of individual or collective resilience or growth. When we gathered again, each person added something to our circle that represented their connection to the place and the land. Children's drawings, flowers, and a list of everyone who helped build The Center were included.

Each day, after spending a few minutes grounding and centering together, we focused on exploring a different sense. During our first exploration, which is called *Boundaries* and is inspired by an activity developed by Schechner, we used the following instructions:

1. Find a spot in the space that calls you. That is your "home." Sense or mark its boundaries.

2. Spend time getting to know your home. Examine it with each of your senses, separately. Look. Smell. Listen. Feel. Taste. Move. Imagine.

3. One person silently travels from their home to each person's home. As they make their way, there is emergent interaction with each person and their home. When they are done, they return to their own home. The next person will then make a tour of each person's home.

4. When not traveling or being visited in one's home, witness the emergent, dyadic interactions occurring between people in different homes.

After I instructed each person to find a spot, their "home," we spent several quiet minutes smelling, gazing, listening, touching, and moving. One person was at the edge of a labyrinth, another near a crabapple tree, a third among flowers and grass, and I was in an overgrown sandbox. Next, each person, one at time, travelled a route to visit each person in their home. The person being visited welcomed in the traveler, non-verbally, and showed, non-verbally, something about their home: the smell of bark, the warmth of the sun while lying on the grass, the vista from a ridge, or a tiny apple tree growing at the edge of their space. Those who weren't traveling or welcoming witnessed the interactions.

The entire, silent activity took about one hour to complete, and afterward we had loads of "data" to debrief and make meaning from. Some people welcomed each person that visited in exactly the same way; others changed what they did, depending on who visited. As we watched how different people welcomed others into their "homes," we noted how we each might do our own welcoming differently.

Another day, to explore image and symbolic sense, I adapted Augusto Boal's activity *The Great Game of Power*.[31] Instructed to silently sculpt six folding chairs, a table, and a water bottle into the image of "a place together," each person created their own image, again witnessed by others. After a round of individual sculpting, I invited participants to literally build on each other's ideas, to sculpt together, iteratively and silently. Chairs were stacked willy nilly, formed a line, or leaned into each other. The table was flipped over and became a cradle with a "baby"—the bottle—placed precariously on top of chairs, or ignored. The bottle was at the center, lying down, or opened. Again, we had much to talk about when it came time to debrief and share meaning. We also explored our visceral senses (smell, taste, gut) with an eating meditation, and we closed our week together with a future-visioning activity that gave us an opportunity to synthesize our work and dream forward.

Later, Eleanor described the communal healing and connection the group experienced during our time together: "You awaken people. I see you as a healer. When we were doing that exercise where we were sitting in different areas and going to people's houses, the way you were watching created connective tissue."

As we saw, the *Boundaries* activity, which Eleanor described, involves a participant exploring their space, connecting with other participants in an emergent fashion, learning, changing, and going back "home." It is an embodied metaphor of a transformation journey. A group finds their way in an iterative journey of explosion and integration and explosion and integration. My role as Organizational Performance Artist is to offer a structure and to watch, to hold the mirror that allows for communal thriving and liberation to be experienced, seen, named, and integrated.

My work with Orchard Hill was not so terribly different from the Organizational Performance Art I had been doing prior to the pandemic, but our collective endurance of not working together in person and the centering of the physical body and space over our talking heads and minds created different outcomes. In the following weeks, back in Brooklyn, I savored the magic that had occurred, and I began to adapt the work we had done to work I was doing with other groups, still in the Zoom room. It would be quite some more time before in-person facilitation would happen on a regular basis; however, my approach to inviting in joy and possibility was broadening, adapting to the times we were living in.

COMING TO OUR SENSES, TOGETHER, ONLINE

"We need team building." When a human rights group reached out to me, I was warned that their staff, who spanned three continents and four time zones, were so fried from working exclusively with virtual technologies that the organization's norm was to keep their video cameras off during Zoom meetings unless it was absolutely necessary to turn them on. They were mired in the existential abyss of enduring the global pandemic for nearly two years, not to mention the many different social, economic, and ecological disasters affecting where they each lived or came from.

I agreed to work with them if they could agree to work together in a different way. We could keep the cameras off most of the time; however, I wanted to center activities that would awaken the senses, similar to the live work I had done with Orchard Hill, only using virtual technologies. Were they up for that? "Yes!" they thirstily replied.

I Zoomed with this group for four days in a row. After the first day of talking to black rectangles with names in the middle, I was in despair, wondering how I could possibly help build community and cohesion. Over the days, I slowly introduced sensory activities that invited participants to be grounded in their actual, physical spaces and to share with one another. I led a version of *Boundaries*, this time with dyads, that involved first engaging in an exploration of whatever physical space they were in and then silently sharing with a partner. I also facilitated eating meditations and sensory explorations of items from nature.

We talked about how, prior to the pandemic, people wanted to be able to work on their own, asynchronously, and how the pandemic produced a palpable hunger for being together in person, and yet how overwhelming it was to gather again, as we began to engage in large group meetings. One participant described one of the first in-person events they went to during the pandemic:

> There were about ten organizers in a group of about sixty. Every organizer was exhausted. It was twice the work and twice the money to bring people together compared to the before times. Participants found it overstimulating and didn't know how to engage with people.

Toward the end of the week, participants were keeping their cameras on, long after the short allotted times I had asked them to do so. Folks opened up, tears flowed, and so did laughter. We had honest conversations about Zoom fatigue and of the fantasies we were holding of getting back to how things were before the pandemic. We let go of the idea that there was a new normal we should be holding our breath for, and we began to accept the moment we were in. This allowed us to adapt and be in reality. We could continue to move toward communal thriving and liberation, creatively using the tools that kept us safe.

As we closed our time together and marveled at the greater sense of community we had developed, as well as muscle for continuing to work during constantly changing, unpredictable times, we discussed how staff can continue to use embodied, sensory activities among themselves as well as with the people and groups they support. "How can we flow with these times, rather than fight them?" I asked.

One person offered the idea of going back to the asynchronous and very concrete delight of sending and receiving actual physical letters. Another person floated the idea of going back to conference calls, a technology that had been immediately ditched, despite its utility, at the beginning of the pandemic. Unlike video technologies, telephone calls allow people to fully participate while using their bodies however they'd like:

Participant: Old school conference calls could be good! People can walk.

Alissa: That's leadership!

Participant: Going back to the "old" ways.

Zooming for twelve hours over four mornings was a lot. It was not unlike the four meetings, each two to three hours long, that I had facilitated live with Orchard Hill. Both filled folks up quite a bit. When people gathered, whether it was in person or virtually, we needed to do so from a place of understanding that we were in a different place since the pandemic had uprooted our lives. A little bit of stimulation went a long way. Our sensory deprivation had made us extra sensitive to the inputs that we received. We juiced them, savored them, learned from them. We filled easily, and we also needed space and downtime. We learned we could work less hard, together. We learned that we could heal.

As we finished out the second year of the global pandemic, I centered my Organizational Performance Art with organizations and communities on a delicate holding of space for joy and possibility, a space where people could mourn what had been lost, revisit the fantasy of coming back together the way we used to, and creatively adapt to what would be next.

ORGANIZATIONAL ART/ PERFORMANCE ART

A YEAR AFTER MY SENSORY WORK WITH ORCHARD HILL, I HAD the opportunity to spend a few weeks there, living in community. Eleanor ran a summer camp on the land, and I took over her bread delivery route so she could focus on the kids. The bread is from Orchard Hill Breadworks, an artisanal bakery run by her son Noah that sources local ingredients and serves much of southern New Hampshire and Vermont.

My delivery route crisscrossed the Connecticut River, taking me to about a dozen small towns to deliver fresh-baked deliciousness to small village stores and farmstands. There were many details I had to master in a short time: from packing the van efficiently, to learning the route, to knowing how to display the goods so they would sell well, to remembering extra details like picking up produce to use for Breadworks' community fundraising pizza nights.

After my first few runs, I sensed the neurons in my brain making new connections as I learned the country roads. I even started to improvise my route when I would make some inevitable mistake and need to rejigger it. For someone who trucks with words and group process, it felt amazing to handle bread and a van, to be of concrete service to the larger community.

Earlier that summer, I had the great pleasure of providing consultative support to Bread and Puppet Theater. During my week performing with them in New York City the prior winter, I had had conversations with younger, newer puppeteers who, upon hearing my history with the group and practice in organizational culture building, shared with me their desire to engage in group process with puppeteers who had been with Bread and Puppet for a longer time. They wanted to develop a shared understanding of how to be an anti-racist theater group and level up in their practices of diversity and inclusion.

A few months later, after they participated in an Uprooting White Supremacy workshop given by the worker-owned facilitation cooperative AORTA,[32] I spent time with them unpacking their learning and helping them develop next steps for moving forward. A puppeteer wrote me afterward, "Thank you so much for being such a wonderful facilitator. You allowed us to engage and hold space for hard discussions in a way that was deeply meaningful and transformative." What a rich and full circle I've had the opportunity to partake in, practicing Organizational Performance Art in the service of communal thriving and liberation with this group that first showed me the relationship between performance and social justice!

Another transformative event occurred that summer, as well. While at Orchard Hill, I created an original theater piece for the first time in nearly twenty-five years. Titled *Bread & Bread*,[33] it was a meditation on learning my bread route and my changing history with Bread and Puppet Theater. I began the work with singing my personal anthem for joy and possibility, a shape-note piece called *Captain Kidd* that is adapted and sung at Bread and Puppet pageants:

> Through all the world below
> Light is seen all around
> Search hills and valleys through

There it's found

The growing of the corn
The lily and the thorn
The pleasant and forlorn
All declare light is there
In the meadows dressed in green
There it's seen

Then let my station be
Here on earth, as I see
The sacred one in we
All agree

Through all the world is made
The forest and the glade
Nor let me be afraid
Though I dwell on the hill
Since nature's works declare
Light is there

I performed *Bread & Bread* twice, including a short, Bread and Puppet-inspired flag running, while sharing a story which appeared earlier in this book:

Egg and I ran with our flags, following puppeteers in and out
and around the circus ring. We ran with the flags that have
opened and closed the circus over its many decades,
bright-colored banners hoisted high, illustrating and invoking
the elementals: brother toothbrush, brother sky, sister coffee,
brother frying pan, sister garden, sister wind, brother mountain,
sister water. We ran and ran and ran and ran flags. Really, there's
nothing more joyful for me than running flags at Bread and
Puppet. It makes my heart burst wide, wide, wide open. The

clouds, the sky, the fields, the birds, the grasshoppers, the people, the flags.

I dubbed the platform tent I had been living in the Wall Tent Theater and used the grassy area in front of it as both installation site and audience seating. The piece included a bread pack dance and a lecture on how to efficiently load a delivery van. Blue cloth ran down the middle of the grass, signifying the Connecticut River that flows between New Hampshire and Vermont. As I unfurled red ribbon for weaving among the signs I created to signify the many farmstands and village stores on my route, I mused and wondered about the various people I met or didn't meet on the way:

> Celia gets one little loaf of bread. I don't quite understand the trade because it sounds to me like Orchard Hill gets a cow for bread. That's cool. Celia gets her bread, we get a cow. She's so lucky! She gets a personal delivery service. I have lots of wonderings about Celia: who she is, what she looks like. You know what? I've never opened the bag! I've never looked in to see: Is it the same bread every week? Does she get different ones? Celia's a real mystery to me.

Bread & Bread was a deep, funny, site-specific work for a very specific audience: Orchard Hill bakers and community members. I shared a part of me—my theater performer self—and enlivened the land in a new way. I embodied and welcomed in the joy and possibility of anyone making art from anything anywhere, in the service of community. It was a mirroring back of what I had imbibed, a song of gratitude. Folks were moved, energized, and inspired. They felt seen. I was moved, energized, and inspired. I felt seen, as well.

It was a perfect summer of Organizational Performance Art. I did organizational art with Bread and Puppet. And I did performance art with Orchard Hill. Bread and Bread.

The morning after performing, I woke up and took myself to breakfast at the South Acworth Village Store, a community-run cooperative down the road. I was awash with ideas and excitement. Maybe I would come back and create seasonal works on different parts of the land. Maybe I would craft a new consultative offering where I am in an immersive residence with an organization or community for a few weeks and then create a performance that feeds back to them. Call it "Outside In."

I don't know what's next in my practice of Organizational Art and Performance Art. What I do know is it was liberating to activate my theater performance artist self again and witness its impact. Eleanor marveled at the intimacy of both my consultative and creative work. "That was me, speaking through you," she said, "I see you seeing me seeing you, I feel you feeling me feeling you." I saw in that exact moment a core purpose of Organizational Performance Art: mirroring back, elevating, and making sacred the mundane parts of social functioning that center communal thriving and liberation and making mundane the sacred parts of social functioning that center thriving and liberation.

REFERENCES

WORKS CONSULTED

Arbus, Doon (1973). *Alice in Wonderland: The Forming of a Company and the Making of a Play.* New York: Merlin House.

Artaud, Antonin (1958). *Theater and Its Double.* New York: Grove Press.

Barrett, Frank. "Social Constructionist Challenge to Representational Knowledge: Implications for Understanding Organization Change," in Bushe, G.R., & Marshak, R.J., eds. (2015), *Dialogic Organization Development: The Theory and Practice of Transformational Change.* San Francisco: Berrett-Koehler.

Boal, Augusto (1992). *Games for Actors and Non-Actors.* New York: Routledge.

Gay, Ross (2019). *The Book of Delights.* Chapel Hill, NC: Algonquin Books.

Goldberg, Roselee (1988). *Performance Art: From Futurism to the Present.* New York: Harry N. Abrams.

Grotowski, Jerzy (1968). *Towards a Poor Theatre.* New York: Simon and Schuster.

Kaprow, Allan (1966). *Assemblage, Environments, & Happenings*. New York: H.N. Abrams.

Lebell, Sharon (1995). *The Art of Living: The Classic Manual on Virtue, Happiness, and Effectiveness/Epictetus: A New Interpretation*. San Francisco: HarperSanFrancisco.

Nichols, Peter (1972). *A Day in the Death of Joe Egg*. New York: Samuel French.

Okun, Tema (2021). *What Is White Supremacy Culture?* https://www.whitesupremacyculture.info/what-is-it.html.

Rosenthal, Caitlin. "Plantations Practiced Modern Management," *Harvard Business Review,* September 2013.

Schechner, Richard (1973). *Environmental Theater*. New York: Hawthorn Books.

Schechner, Richard (2020) *Performance Studies: An Introduction*, 4th Edition. New York: Routledge.

WORKS BY THE AUTHOR

Schwartz, Alissa (1991). *Made in the CFA: An Ensemble's Environmental Performance*. Middleton, CT: Wesleyan University. (BA honors thesis.)

Schwartz, Alissa (2008). *Stayers, Fence-Sitters, and Leavers: Foster Care Workers' Psychological Responses in the Workplace.* New York: Columbia University. (PhD dissertation.)

Schwartz, Alissa (2011). "Foster care workers' emotional responses to their work," *Journal of Sociology and Social Welfare.*

Schwartz, Alissa (2022). *Bread & Bread.* https://vimeo.com/741465340/4df6701635

WEBSITES

A.K. Rice Institute for the Study of Social Systems: www.akriceinstitute.org

AORTA: https://aorta.coop/

The Art of Hosting: https://artofhosting.org/

Center for the Study of Groups and Social Systems: www.csgss.org

Circle Practice: https://peerspirit.com/

Open Space: https://openspaceworld.org/wp2/

Presencing Institute: https://www.presencing.org

The Soul Healing Way: www.soulhealingway.com

Wikipedia's definition of Social Constructionism: https://en.wikipedia.org/wiki/Social_constructionism

World Cafe: http://www.theworldcafe.com/

INTERVIEWS CONDUCTED

Eleanor Elbers (October 9–11 and December 16, 2021)

ENDNOTES

1. Schechner, R. (1973). *Environmental Theater,* New York: Hawthorn Books, p. vii.

2. Schwartz, A. (2008). *Stayers, Fence-Sitters, and Leavers: Foster Care Workers' Psychological Responses in the Workplace.* Columbia University, New York (PhD dissertation). See also: Schwartz, A. (2011). "Foster care workers' emotional responses to their work." *Journal of Sociology and Social Welfare.*

3. Schechner, R. (2020). *Performance Studies: An Introduction,* 4th Edition. New York: Routledge, p. 4.

4. Goldberg, R. (1988). *Performance Art: From Futurism to the Present,* New York: Harry N. Abrams, p. 9.

5. Kaprow, A. (1965). *Assemblage, Environments & Happenings.* New York: Harry N. Abrams.

6. http://www.theworldcafe.com/

7. https://openspaceworld.org/wp2/

8. https://peerspirit.com/

9. Kaprow, A. (1965). *Assemblage, Environments & Happenings.* New York: Harry N. Abrams.

10. Nichols, P. (1972). *A Day in the Death of Joe Egg.* New York: Samuel French.

11. Arbus, D. (1973). *Alice in Wonderland: The Forming of a Company and the Making of a Play.* New York: Merlin House.

12. Quotes from: Schwartz, A. (1991). *Made in the CFA: An Ensemble's Environmental Performance.* Middleton, CT: Wesleyan University.

13. Schwartz, A. (2008). *Stayers, Fence-Sitters, and Leavers: Foster Care Workers' Psychological Responses in the Workplace.* Columbia University, New York (PhD dissertation). See also: Schwartz, A. (2011). "Foster care workers' emotional responses to their work." *Journal of Sociology and Social Welfare.*

14. Schechner, R. (1973). *Environmental Theater.* New York: Hawthorn Books.
15. https://artofhosting.org/
16. https://en.wikipedia.org/wiki/Social_constructionism
17. Barrett, F. "Social Constructionist Challenge to Representational Knowledge: Implications for Understanding Organization Change," in Bushe, G.R., & Marshak, R.J., eds. (2015), *Dialogic Organization Development: The Theory and Practice of Transformational Change.* San Francisco: Berrett-Koehler.
18. Gay, R. (2019). *The Book of Delights.* Chapel Hill, NC: Algonquin Books.
19. Lebell, S. (1995). *The Art of Living: The Classic Manual on Virtue, Happiness, and Effectiveness/Epictetus: A New Interpretation.* San Francisco: HarperSanFrancisco.
20. www.akriceinstitute.org
21. www.csgss.org
22. Schechner, R. (1973). *Environmental Theater.* New York: Hawthorn Books.
23. Okun, T. (2021) *What Is White Supremacy Culture?* https://www.whitesupremacyculture.info/what-is-it.html
24. Rosenthal, C. "Plantations Practiced Modern Management," *Harvard Business Review,* September 2013.
25. Artaud, A. (1958). *Theater and Its Double.* New York: Grove Press, p. 13.
26. www.soulhealingway.com
27. Schechner, R. (1973). *Environmental Theater.* New York: Hawthorn Books.
28. Schechner, R. (1973). *Environmental Theater.* New York: Hawthorn Books.
29. Grotowski, J. (1968). *Towards a Poor Theatre.* New York: Simon and Schuster.
30. Boal, A. (1992). *Games for Actors and Non-Actors.* New York: Routledge.
31. Boal, A. (1992). *Games for Actors and Non-Actors.* New York: Routledge.
32. https://aorta.coop/
33. *Bread & Bread:* https://vimeo.com/741465340/4df6701635

ACKNOWLEDGMENTS

THERE ARE SO MANY FOLKS WHO SUPPORTED ME AS I WORKED on this book. I want to especially share big gratitude to...

Andrew Drury, Ash Drury and Egg Drury. Thank you, thank you, thank you to my life partner who co-published this work and to my awesome kids. You heard me talk (aka whine!) about this work for a few years and cheered me on and made sure I knew I got this. I grew into a book writer in our home together.

April Schwartz. Mom, I had no idea that writing this would be a way to connect with you as a fellow writer. We are more alike than I realized, and I so enjoy communing with you, both when you were in the seen world and now that you are in the spirit realm.

Patrick Barber. Thank you for being my kickass designer and publishing partner. You have been an endless, aligned joy to work with. Thank you for the spot-on, thoughtful design, hours of support and advice, and big laughs. I look forward to our next collaboration!

Helen Klonaris, Susan Misra, and James Wright. A thousand thanks, Susan, for writing the ForeForeword and to all three of you for reading earlier, messier iterations of this work and giving me such thoughtful feedback and encouragement. You were my adhoc writers group, even if you didn't know it!

Eleanor Elbers and Rose Jonas. Thank you for being in deep relationship with me and caring so much about me and my writing. Your pure excitement over my work makes me feel held and loved.

Jackie Yodashkin. You helped me claim this project. Thank you for helping me organize my initial thoughts and coaching me through the terror of throwing my hat in the ring.

Alex Cruden and Nancy Rawlinson. Thank you for your editorial wisdom. You helped me cut, revise, order, and scrub.

ABOUT THE AUTHOR

PHOTO BY LIZ LIGON

Alissa Schwartz, MSW, PhD, Principal of Solid Fire Consulting, is a master facilitator and organizational culture builder with over 25 years of experience working with groups. She is co-editor and chapter author of a special issue of *New Directions in Evaluation* that focuses on the intersectionalities of evaluation and facilitation and holds a doctorate from Columbia University, where she studied organizational psychology and behavior.

In an earlier iteration of her ongoing fascination with group process, Alissa created and directed avant-garde theater and performance. This early influence sneakily shows up in her current consulting work, as well.

Alissa is based out of Lenapehoking/Brooklyn, where she parents, grandparents, bikes, practices yoga, and occasionally performs with Bread & Puppet Theater and in her own work. Learn more about her work and writing at www.solidfireconsulting.com.